From Silence to Stories

By Emily Getzfreid

From Silence to Stories

Copyright © 2017 by Emily Getzfreid

Cover Photo: Kandi McClure Photography
Cover Design: Freddie Robles
Interior Design: Erica Smith, Ebook Conversions

ISBN: 978-0-692-96735-5

Author's Note

The stories in this book are told with permission. Names and identifying details have been changed. Additionally, this work focuses on the prevalence and impact of sexual abuse among female survivors. While I recognize that many males also experience sexual abuse in childhood, addressing those experiences is outside the scope of this book.

A Special Thank You

To the sexual abuse and assault survivors who participated in this project: thank you for trusting me with your stories.

– Emily

Table of Contents

• •

Dearest Denial
How tightly to you we cling
What influence you wield
Over our weak, weak minds
"He could never do something like that!
Obviously, she's lying."
And on and on
We wear you
Like a blanket on a frosty night
Shivering but grateful
For your brand of truth

Then years from now, weary with silence
Desperate to function in her dysfunctional world
Even there you'll reign
"I'm over that. It's been 20 years!"
But at night:
"I'll never be free."

How successfully you've helped us
Deny the darkness

Yet, powerful as you are, you don't work alone
Dearest Deceit is your lifelong friend
Lovers of hate, you whisper together:
"You're the only one.
No one will understand.

Your fault.
Your fault.
Your fault."

But worse! You curse generations
From mother to child to child to child:
"It happened to me and I turned out fine.
Every girl goes through it.
She'll get used to it.
He'll leave me.
Leave me.
Me."

Oh, but yet…
For all your power, still you are weak
Your enemy is greater than you ever hoped to be
Glorious Truth, stomp Denial like a snake!
Writhing and hissing and ready to die
May Deceit suffer the wrath of your light
Truth! I pray you be louder
Be louder
Be LOUDER!

Intervene
Interfere
Invade

Where light shines in the darkness,
The darkness cannot overcome it

Part I

Prologue

The heavy oak doors open and a young girl enters the courtroom. Her blond hair, falling past her shoulder blades, shines like the polished wood railing of the jury box she walks past. Her eyes are downcast, her face pale and carefully blank. She is well dressed and meticulously groomed, though as she pointed out to her mother that morning, the lace trimming at the bottom of her powder-blue skirt doesn't quite match the lace at the collar of her striped blouse. But her mom had told her not to worry about it. *No one will notice,* she'd said, nervously fidgeting with the buttons of her own blouse.

No one will notice.

And of course, her mom was right. The courtroom is packed, but not with people who cared one whit about the girl's appearance. The prosecutor and defense attorney are much more concerned with the presentation of her testimony: Will she tell the truth? Will she stick to the facts? Will she be a convincing witness? The spectators – a sea of them – are made up of supporters on both sides of the aisle. Some are the shocked and skeptical family of the accused, convinced the girl is lying, that she has somehow been coerced into making up her ghastly story to satisfy her mother's desire for revenge. Others are the girl's family, angered by what she has already been forced to endure, worried about how she will make it through the day. Together they make up one large extended family, divided by divorce, bitterness, and an outright refusal to see beyond the perspective of their own narrowed eyes.

After a seeming eternity, the girl reaches the witness stand, swears to *tell the truth, the whole truth, and nothing but the truth*, and takes her seat. Knowing she can avoid it no longer, she lifts her eyes for the first time. She finds her mother in the crowd first, sitting behind the railing at the back of the courtroom. She next sees the prosecutor, already rising from his chair at the table to her left, and then the defense attorney sitting directly before her. Finally, she turns her eyes to her father, sitting at the defense table.

He looks the same as always, she thinks, noticing his thinning gray hair, salt and pepper beard, and gold-rimmed glasses. His face is gentle, his return gaze benign. She realizes again that he doesn't *look* like a child molester. He looks like a nice man. A good father. A normal person.

Confused by her thoughts, her gaze lights upon him only for a moment. Thankfully, the prosecutor is already beginning to ask her questions. As the sole witness to the crimes being prosecuted, the girl has neither the time nor the courage to study the man she loves and doesn't love, fears but doesn't fear, hates but could not possibly hate. She cannot consider the possible consequences of her testimony – her father's imprisonment and all it may entail – because if she did, her mouth might refuse to speak.

Her words might refuse to come.

Her lungs might refuse to breathe.

Instead, she can only turn her eyes to the prosecutor, be encouraged by his encouraging smile, open her mouth –

And tell her story.

Shamed into Silence

Twenty years later the story of that day is one I have never told before. As I look back on it now, only a few details remain crisp in my memory: lying on the floor in an empty courtroom, coloring in a brand-new book, as I waited my turn to testify; the defense attorney's terrible plaid suit, at least twenty years out of date; my dad's face looking the same as always. The rest of the courtroom is indistinct in my mind, its edges softened by two decades of intentional inattention.

At the time, my thirteen-year-old self had wanted nothing more than to forget any of it ever happened, so I don't think I ever spoke of it again after the jury handed down their verdict. I never spoke of it to my mom and step-dad, who likely believed talking about it would stir up emotions best left unfelt. Nor to my brothers, with whom I've never had another conversation about our father even now. And not to my friends, because having testified against your father in a criminal rape case doesn't often come up in the course of teenage conversation. It doesn't come up in any conversation, really, so I've continued to keep it to myself.

Until now, of course, because the time for keeping silent has long passed.

Like most child sexual abuse survivors, I've kept some of the specifics of my story – like the day I testified

the time for keeping silent has long passed

– to myself. Unlike most survivors, however, I've had the opportunity to tell my story in general terms as a church retreat speaker many times. Standing before groups of women of all ages, I've told how my dad began molesting me when I was nine, that within a few months the abuse turned to rape and continued until he was arrested two years later. My first time as a retreat speaker, I told only the bare bones: molestation, rape, arrest, plus a little of what came after. Promiscuity in high school, sexual dysfunction in marriage. I told only what I was sure other women, both sexual abuse survivors and those who had never experienced sexual abuse, could identify with. From the first time I shared, though, women would come to me afterward and thank me for being so open. They didn't know how much I held back, but for them it didn't matter. They responded as though my story was the one they'd been waiting their whole lives to hear.

And sadly, it was.

Because they'd never heard anyone talk about being sexually abused before.

Because they'd never told a soul about their own experience.

Because hearing me tell even a truncated version of my story was the permission they needed to tell their own.

As retreats passed, the telling got easier. The more times I told my story, the more I was *able* to tell, until I was able to share all of it – not just what happened to me, but how I had felt about it and how those feelings impacted my behavior. Eventually, I was able to own the things I had always held back: the shame I felt, not about what had been done to me, but about what *I* had done in response, and everything I felt my actions said about me.

Like my belief that I was, ultimately, unlovable.

Irredeemable.

Destined to live under the cloud of my abuse experience for the rest of my life.

"*Twenty years,*" I told them the last time I spoke. "It's been twenty years that this thing has been controlling me. Today is the day I shine a light on it, expose all of it, because I refuse to let it control me anymore."

Finally telling the *whole truth* elicited an incredible response in the room. Nearly every woman came forward at the end for prayer and personal ministry, not because they were all abuse survivors, but because all of us have incidents from our past that we've hidden out of fear and shame. We've all been held hostage by lies we've believed about ourselves. That day, many women reached the end of their willingness to accept those lies any longer.

They came forward. They told their stories. And by doing so, they stepped onto the path to freedom and healing.

There in that setting – a church retreat filled with like-minded people of the same faith, people committed to the growth, prosperity, and healing of one another – it's okay to talk about the subjects we all religiously avoid in the outside world. My church's retreats are a safe place, an opportunity to get real about things like pornography, sexual addiction, and sexual abuse. They are a place to *know*, without doubt, that we will be supported, loved, and cared for no matter what we reveal.

An exception – that's what those retreats are. Because we all go back to the real world when the weekend is over, the world that millions and millions of other sexual abuse survivors live in every day, a world that offers little respite from the weight of the stories we carry. In the real world, the vast majority of adult sexual abuse survivors have never spoken of their experiences aloud. For some the stories remain traumatic, eliciting the same flight, fight, or freeze response as did the actual event, even decades later. For others, their stories are simply locked away – never opened, never owned, their destructive power never acknowledged in any way. Their stories are the monsters beneath their beds, feeding on their shame, growing more powerful as the years pass.

Monsters thrive in darkness.

The stigma of sexual abuse demands that survivors live in silence, keeping their monsters a secret, never turning on the light.

Yet assuming the typical survivor wanted or even *needed* to share her story, whom would

the stigma of sexual abuse demands that survivors live in silence

she tell? So few want to hear it. Therapists. Perhaps a close friend. Counselors and ministers in the business of healing. To the rest of the world, pained and discomfited by its contents, her story is thought best untold. Despite our culture's fixation with tragedies packaged for us by the media, real, *personal* stories of abuse and trauma make us uncomfortable. They grieve and anger us, make us feel defenseless against the tyrannical evil of the world in which we live. Stories of sexual abuse do that and more: they repulse us – *all of us*, whether we've experienced sexual abuse or not. They leave us feeling dirty and powerless. Even I, an ardent advocate for sexual abuse awareness and prevention, someone who understands the soul-cleansing power of storytelling – even I avoid it whenever possible. During my last semester of college, the same semester in which I began writing this book, I had to read a case study about a boy who, from age 4 to 11, had endured some of the vilest, most abhorrent abuse acts I have ever heard. At 17, several years removed from his abuse, he told his story in the case study matter-of-factly, attempting to hide his brokenness behind an objective list of the acts perpetrated against him.

I admit that I did not just hate reading his story. I *loathed* it. I did not want to analyze his experience, didn't want to examine the ways his life had been affected by the trauma. Truthfully, hearing his story hurt me. As he was someone I did not know and could not help, I felt that the pain his story caused me was needless, unnecessary. I closed my heart to it, pretended his story was a work of fiction, and refused to let it touch me.

Keep silent, young man, so that you do not break my heart.

But as long as I'm being honest with myself, what would my response have said to him?

Keep silent, young man, so that you do not break my heart.

The freedom and healing you may find by telling your story are not worth the pain it causes me.

If he had been standing before me telling his story, he would have looked into my eyes and seen horror. Disgust. Repulsion.

And he would have been shamed into silence.

I can picture him now, this man I've never met: eyes shuttered, heart resigned, he steps into the cage my demand for his silence built for him.

Because that's what silence does: it binds.

It entraps.

It stacks like the bricks of prison walls and shuts the survivor in.

While those walls protect the rest of us from facing the disturbing reality of sexual abuse, the survivor within is held in some tortuous limbo, both desperate to break free and mortally terrified of doing so, as the weight of the walls – the weight of their unspoken story – becomes more and more difficult to bear. The survivor remains trapped within the claustrophobic confines of their silence, fully convinced that it's the only way.

Not just because the stories themselves feel impossible to share, which they do.

But also because they live in a society unwilling to hear them, a society that has closed its eyes and ears in a frantic attempt to pretend them away.

With this book and these stories, I hope to change that.

Though I write from the perspective of a childhood sexual abuse survivor, all of us, whether we are survivors or not, are vulnerable to being deceived about sexual abuse. Silence makes that deception easy. The lack of conversation on the topic allows us to spend our whole lives without ever even acknowledging what we believe. some would even argue that they do not, in fact, have thoughts and beliefs about sexual abuse. To them I would say, *Yes, you do.*

We *all* do.

And they are more powerful than you think.

The next few chapters will examine some of those beliefs and how they affect the way we parent, our interactions with others, and the judgements we make. We'll explore more fully what silence does. We'll see how some survivors and non-survivors alike have overcome their deceptions, how others remain trapped by them, and how still others are slowly breaking down the walls that years of silence have built around them.

My hope and prayer is that the child sexual abuse survivor who reads this book will find the courage to dig deep into their story, to confront its lies, and to speak up about their experiences. I pray that the non-survivor, the person who has never experienced sexual abuse in any form, is encouraged to listen with their whole heart. May we all begin to ask the questions for which we desperately need the answers: Who are the victims of sexual abuse? Who are the perpetrators? What can I do to protect my children and extended family? What can I do to help the adults in my life who survived sexual abuse in childhood to thrive?

To get there, we'll have to resolve not to put the subject aside and walk away when it gets too uncomfortable – which it will, countless times. We must be willing to examine and admit our beliefs about sexual abuse, even when those beliefs are different than we thought they'd be. Finally, we must be willing to embrace the daunting reality of child sexual abuse and to share that truth with others.

By telling our stories.

By listening.

By creating an atmosphere in our society in which shame, guilt, and silence have no place.

Together, we can break the cycle of sexual abuse.

We must only begin.

Stripping Silence of Power

In the weeks and months before my father's trial, I worked with the district attorney, a nice woman named Renee, to build the case. The first thing she asked me to do was write a statement describing everything that had happened, to the best of my ability. Renee told me, "Just seal it in an envelope and put it in your mom's purse. She'll make sure I get it." My dismay must have been clear on my face because she said, "She won't read it if you don't want her to." My mom, sitting next to me, nodded in agreement.

"I don't want her to read it," I said quickly, thinking *I don't want anyone to read it. I don't even want to write it.*

But I did, describing the abuse in the only way I knew: teenage slang. I wrote down everything my dad had ever done to me, acts for which I had never heard the proper terms, and so could only describe using the offensive and degrading language of youth who believe that slang makes them sound more mature. I still cringe when I remember some of the things I wrote, especially when I consider how many people were forced to read it. The prosecutor, the defense attorney, the investigators. My mom, who I later learned did read it before turning it over to the D.A. How must they have felt, reading my words?

Surely no one involved in a child rape case can escape un-traumatized.

The D.A. had advised me to write my story in general terms, but to also share specific instances of abuse. It was not enough to say that my dad had been abusing me for about two years; the charges filed against him had to refer to specific acts and the exact date on which they occurred. I didn't understand what that meant, of course. They told me to make a list of dates, so I did, using a calendar to determine which days I had been at my dad's. I wrote down nine dates and next to each date I wrote one of two words: rape or molestation. I was told to study that list, to memorize it because it would be the crux of my testimony.

I never even looked at it again, except on the day the D.A. commandeered an empty courtroom so I could practice my testimony a few days before the trial. During the trial itself I was questioned and questioned again about the dates I had provided. Somehow, despite my refusal to study the list, I messed up only one date, stating that what had happened on that date was molestation when I had written "rape" in my statement.

Looking back, I wonder if I would have provided more than one or two dates if I had understood that each date would correspond with a sixty-year sentence. I had done everything the court asked of me – writing my statement, visiting the gynecologist, practicing my testimony – while of two minds: knowing I was doing the right thing but always wishing, *yearning*, to take it back. Despite all, I loved my dad. My thirteen-year-old heart didn't want anything bad to happen to him. I was afraid of all the ways our lives had changed since his arrest and afraid of the unknowable changes that were still to come. In the end, the charge that corresponded with the date I messed up was thrown out, but the jury found him guilty on all others: eight counts of injury to a minor child.

Four hundred and twenty years plus life.

Four hundred and twenty years plus life.

I couldn't have known it at the time, but it didn't matter how many charges he was convicted of; he would only live to serve the slightest fraction of his sentence. He was found dead, murdered in his prison cell, a mere eight months after his conviction.

Out of all that took place between the first day I told someone about the abuse I was experiencing and the last day of my dad's trial, one thing has had the power to haunt me – to control me, to shape my beliefs and attitudes about myself like nothing else. A single question, asked by a desperate public defender in a bad suit.

"Did you ever enjoy what your father did to you?"

I remember the shock I felt at the question. The betrayal. After everything that had happened – my own testimony, my father's confession, the doctor's description of the physical injury to my body – this grown man had the nerve to ask if I had *enjoyed* being sexually abused?

"No!" I replied, unable to hide my disgust, not just at the question but at the man who asked it.

Yet, the reason the question haunted me for so long wasn't in the question itself. It was in my answer.

Saying "no" was the only lie I told that day.

As a thirteen-year-old girl, I had no way of knowing that the human body is designed to enjoy sexual stimulation. I did not know that the body isn't cognizant of the violation, of the heinousness of the crime being committed against it, the way the mind and heart are. The human body responds, period. Instead, I knew only that I had felt physical pleasure at times during the abuse. I knew that even though I always refused to willingly participate, I had been curious about the things my dad asked me to do. I had been tempted to do them. And I fully believed that was wrong.

Which, according to thirteen-year-old logic, meant *I* was wrong.

As I got older, I learned the truth about sexual stimulation and that I truly had no control over my body's response. But that knowledge was powerless against what my heart said at the time must be true – that I was culpable. A participant in the abuse, rather than a victim of it.

Years passed. I grew up, got married, and had children – all before my twenty-first birthday. My husband and I recommitted our lives to Christ and became involved in a church that believes the body of Christ should be a safe place to be our true selves, a church that celebrates and embraces the healing power of God. There we met pastors and leaders who were open about their pasts. Abuse, abortion, addiction – none of it is hidden, and the atmosphere of transparency and acceptance made me feel safe to tell my story. It was through this church that I attended my first Encounter retreat. As I listened to Pastor Jean speak on sexual wholeness, I thought, *I can do that*. But even more surprising, *I want to do that*.

I followed the church's discipleship track, became a small group leader, retreat speaker, and eventually a women's ministry leader. But all the while, the feeling that I was a disgusting fraud chewed on my heart. Despite my inward belief that my church truly was a safe place to be real, I could never quite convince myself that it was a safe place for *someone like me*. Other people, yes. People whom God would graciously forgive no matter what they confessed. People with whom others could identify because no matter what they contain, our stories are really not so different in their effect. Broken hearts, broken lives…just waiting to be put back together.

But never me, because I was not one of those people.

I never admitted those feelings to myself or anyone else, of course. Doing so would have required me to confront how disgusting I felt, how ashamed. That shame, deeply repressed but all consuming, was a secret I could not help but deny. I could not admit I even had shame. Doing so would have surely shattered the thin glass shell that was holding me together.

Until one Sunday morning, when my pastor preached a message about breaking free of shame. By then I had been in church for *years*, leading a small group, speaking at retreats, listening to so many others tell their stories – stories of abuse, addiction, and willful sin that always included the shame they felt about what they'd done and what had been done *to* them. I had heard countless messages about how sin and shame were triumphed over at the cross. I had memorized Romans 8:1, "So now there is no condemnation for those who believe in Christ Jesus," and if given the opportunity, I would have told you emphatically that no matter what you've done or what's been done to you, you have no reason to feel ashamed. I would have held your hand and fervently prayed that God would reveal His truth to you, and I would have believed on your behalf that freedom and healing were coming swiftly on the wings of grace.

And I had convinced myself that I believed those things were true. For you, for me, for all of us.

Until that day, when I could pretend no longer.

Why that particular Sunday? What did my pastor say that I hadn't heard before? I have no idea.

Until that day, when I could pretend no longer.

I honestly can't even remember. I just know that whatever he preached about breaking free of shame broke *me*. It broke my ability to suppress and repress and tune out uncomfortable feelings. It broke the walls I had built up to keep out my shame, to keep it hidden and deniable. It broke my will to continue carrying on as if I were *okay* when I knew deep down that I wasn't.

So I cried. Through the last half of the message and all through the altar call at the end, I sobbed as quietly as possible. (I feel sorry for my husband even now. What must he have thought?) I didn't move when the pastor invited the congregation to stand, nor when he called the prayer teams to the front and invited anyone who was in need to come forward for personal ministry. I *couldn't* stand. I felt exposed, as though every person in the room could see the deepest, ugliest parts of my soul. The parts I denied even while I felt they defined me. The parts I feared would consume me if ever they were truly uncovered.

I left the church that day without giving my husband or anyone else the slightest insight into what I was dealing with. I didn't acknowledge my thoughts in any way save one; when I got home, I opened my journal to a new page and wrote two sentences: "Sometimes I enjoyed the things my dad did to me. I've been ashamed of it my whole life."

And then I folded the page over so that I would never have to see the words I'd written. Until writing this now, I've never looked at them again.

The next few weeks were rough. Finally acknowledging the thing that made me most ashamed was a good start, but I had not reached my turning point. I was no longer living in denial of my shame – at least to myself – but I had not yet exposed its lies. Through my stalwart silence, I continued to keep it hidden, giving it even more power to torment me.

Because that's what silence does: it torments.

It vanquishes.

And, ultimately, it subjugates, turning the truth into a lie, and making the survivor a prisoner to it.

How many conversations had I had with other abuse survivors? A hundred, maybe more. Yet never had I heard another person admit to feelings similar to mine. I sincerely believed, based on what I had never heard, that I was the only one weak enough, defective enough to have enjoyed a single moment of the violation that is child sexual abuse.

the only thing capable of stripping silence of its power: a story

It's not surprising, then, that my turning point, when it came, arrived in the only way it could, through the only thing capable of stripping silence of its power: a story.

I was in the car with one of my dearest friends, a woman whose abuse experience I was familiar with, just as she was familiar with mine, when she said, "Pastor's message on shame a few weeks ago really opened my eyes to some things."

"Really?" I asked, thinking of my own written confession. "What kind of things?"

"Well," she said, after a pause. "It made me realize how much shame I felt about what my dad did to me. Sometimes, when he touched me, it felt good. I've always felt disgusted with myself for that."

I don't remember what I said in reply, I just remember the way I felt.

Like a rock-hard band around my chest had cracked, just a little, offering the hope of some future deep breath.

Like a mountainous weight on my shoulders had shifted infinitesimally, yielding the heretofore unfelt anticipation of its eventual falling away.

Though I was still a few years away from throwing off my shame completely, her words reverberated in my heart, ringing out the truth I desperately needed to hear.

I'm not the only one.

Silence, I hope you see, is a liar.

But stories, even in the simplest forms, bring truth.

To Trade Deception for Truth

All of us, those who have experienced sexual abuse and those who haven't, have beliefs about child sexual abuse that impact the way we think and interact with the world. For survivors, those beliefs shape nearly every aspect of our lives. Because we rarely stop to examine them, their influence goes unnoticed, and their power unchallenged. We embrace silence as a form of protection against the reality of our abuse experience. As a result, we can spend our entire lives believing the lies our experience tells us – because that's what silence does.

It deceives.

Like a shroud wrapped tightly around the survivor's heart and mind, silence holds the deceptions about sexual abuse tightly in place. Rather than understanding the truth of sexual abuse and its impact, the survivor understands only condemnation and the false expectations of what she *should* feel. She puts impossible demands upon herself, yet strives to meet them anyway, always to her own detriment. Like breaking an arm but refusing treatment because she believes it shouldn't be broken. She convinces herself the bones will eventually fuse together, then she soldiers on, ignoring the pain, pretending it isn't there. She never allows those around her to know her arm was broken, much less make them aware of the pain she hides. But for the rest of her life, the arm will ache.

Sometimes unbearably.

That is life for many sexual abuse survivors. Silence has taught her that she shouldn't even be feeling the pain. She's never heard what is "normal" for a sexual abuse survivor to experience in adulthood. She assumes her struggles, and the inherent weaknesses they indicate, are hers alone.

Silence tells her, "You're the only one."

Rarely does anyone tell her any different.

Yet here is the truth she urgently needs to hear: those who suffer child sexual abuse (CSA) are more likely to develop post-traumatic stress disorder (PTSD) than victims of any other kind of trauma[1]. They are also more likely to endure *lifelong* PTSD symptoms, even though those same symptoms often naturally abate over time when associated with other forms of trauma[1]. Major depression, anxiety, sexual dysfunction, and suicidal ideation are all considered perfectly normal in adult survivors of CSA[1].

Major depression.

Anxiety.

Sexual dysfunction.

Suicidal thoughts.

They're all *perfectly normal.*

Other normal responses include self-hatred, feelings of guilt and responsibility, eating disorders, lifelong sleep disturbances or insomnia, drug and alcohol abuse, sexual promiscuity, and self-harm[1].

Yet every survivor I've ever spoken with has spent years, if not decades, believing they were *not* normal. When they struggle with depression and low self-worth, they think, *something is wrong with me.* When physical intimacy with the man they love is shadowed by anxiety they can't explain or escape, they think, *I shouldn't feel this way.*

It shouldn't have been a big deal.

It shouldn't still affect me.

I should be strong enough to handle this.

Lies, all of them.

Neither the average abuse survivor nor the non-survivor – one who has never been sexually abused – recognizes the lingering effects of abuse for what they are: the mind's natural response to trauma, unavoidable without early therapeutic intervention[2]. As the natural consequences of sexual abuse play themselves out, survivors and non-survivors alike see the inevitable self-destruction the same way.

Transgression rather than pain.

Weakness rather than wounds.

For the abuse survivor, every bout with depression, every promiscuous sexual encounter, every self-destructive action compounds her shame. She becomes not only a girl who was abused, but a girl who allowed the abuse to dictate her choices for years, if not decades, after it ended. Such personal weakness cannot, to her mind, be forgiven.

Nor even acknowledged.

At least, that's my story, and I've finally learned enough to know I'm not alone in it.

My Story

Sometime after my ninth birthday, I awoke to the foreign feeling of someone's hand between my legs. The hand wasn't moving; it was just *there*, where it shouldn't have been, where it had never been before. I'd been sleeping in my father's bed every other weekend for months, since my parents divorced and my father moved into an apartment. My youngest brother also slept in the bed, while my two older brothers shared the only other bedroom. All of that had begun to feel normal, less like our lives had been ripped apart and more like life moving on.

But the hand – it was new. I lay awake for what felt like hours, stilled beneath the weight of my father's arm around my body and a cold fear that convinced me it would be best to pretend I was still asleep. So I didn't move. Didn't fight. Didn't even try to roll away. I pretended sleep and must have eventually been overtaken by it because when I awoke again the hand was gone. The sun was shining and I was sick to my stomach, but I determined to carry on like nothing was wrong.

That's how it began.

As time went on I would wake again and again to similar things, but it was to get so much worse. Searing, stabbing pain, or sometimes a strange pleasure that I didn't understand in my half-asleep state. Every time I awoke, I went through the same argument in my head: what to do? Fight, scream, run away? Or pretend to sleep? I tried it all. None of it helped for longer than that particular night, because there was always the next night, or the next weekend. He would do it again, over and over, and there was never anything I could do to stop it.

Before long, when my father had progressed from molestation to rape, I began a new tactic: not sleeping. I would lie awake as much of the night as possible, listening for the sound of my father's broken, labored breathing that always foretold what was coming. At the sound of it I might roll as far away as the bed or my sleeping brother would allow. I might get up and hide behind the couch in the living room or under the kitchen table. I might struggle, batting away the hands that reached for me beneath the blanket, but it was fruitless. His arms were strong and he was patient. He'd find me wherever I was, pull me close to him, wrap his arms tightly around me to still my struggle, and wait. I would fall asleep eventually. I always did.

But only because I couldn't help it.

About two years after it began, the abuse ended. Not because I had found a way to fight successfully. Not because my father had suddenly developed a conscience. It ended, in fact, quite by accident. At school one Thursday, I sat in the gym with a couple of friends, Candice and Trisha. Out of the blue, Trisha said, "I bet I have a bigger secret than you do."

Candice didn't say a word, but thinking of the night before, I said, "I doubt it."

Looking nervous and a little angry, Trisha said, "Every time I see my uncle he tries to get me to have sex with him."

Stunned, I looked up at Trisha. My words tumbled out before I could stop them: "The same thing happens to me, but it's not my uncle. It's my dad. And he doesn't just try to get me to have sex with him. He makes me."

This time it was Candice's turn to gasp. Candice had been friends with me a long time, had even spent the night with me at my dad's apartment a few times. I remember one night in particular, when Candice and I were sleeping on a pallet in the other bedroom. My dad came in to get me, grabbing my hand and trying to pull me up to come to bed with him, but I resisted. I knew he wouldn't want to wake Candice, and I was right. Eventually he gave up and went away. The next morning, as he was serving us pancakes at the kitchen table, Candice asked him, "Why did you come in there to get Emily last night?"

I froze in the act of cutting my pancake. I didn't dare look up, but heard my dad say, "Sometimes she comes into my room at night."

Candice, a twelve-year-old with a reputation for being belligerent and disrespectful, refused to let it go. She said, "Yeah, but she didn't last night. You came to get her."

My dad didn't reply, just put the plate full of extra pancakes on the table and left the kitchen, saying, "You guys hurry up and eat. We have to leave in a few minutes." And that was the end of the conversation. Candice and I never talked about it, but I always wondered what Candice would say if she knew the truth.

I didn't have to wonder anymore. Immediately Candice cried out, "Emily, you have to tell somebody!"

"No! I can't tell anyone. And you have to promise you won't tell either." I glared at her, but she refused to back down.

"You have to! You can't let him keep doing that to you."

"Candice, I can't. *No*," I said, cutting off her protest. "I'm not telling anyone."

At that moment the bell rang, signaling the beginning of the day's classes. I hurried away before Candice could say anything else. I was so mad at myself for saying anything. What had I been thinking? I'd never told anyone about what my dad did to me, had never even considered telling anyone. I was sure that he would get into trouble if anyone found out, and I didn't want that. What if something bad happened to him? What if they took him away?

Since the abuse began, I had gotten really good at living in two worlds: daytime and nighttime. I didn't allow the two to mix in my mind; what happened in the night at my dad's never intruded on my thoughts during the day. Once the night was over, I put it out of my mind. It wasn't even hard to do, really, because my dad was a good father in every other way. He never yelled at me or my brothers when he got mad or said mean things to us. He rarely spanked us with a belt like we got at home, or called us names. In fact, he never really got mad at all. He didn't even get mad when he found out that me and my friends in the apartment complex were sneaking cigarettes and smoking behind the building. He just bought me a pack of Marlboros and told me I could only smoke inside. He let me hang out at the movie theater with my friends even though he knew we didn't go in to watch a movie. He basically let me do whatever I wanted and was *nice* about it.

It would be over twenty years before I understood that he had been carefully, intentionally grooming me to accept the abuse. As a child from a broken home – both halves dysfunctional in different ways – I only knew that in one of them I felt safe and loved, while in the other I felt worthless and often afraid. With his kind voice and permissive attitude, my dad represented a safe haven, an escape. But more than that, I felt strangely protective of him. He was a *good dad*, I told myself. He loved his kids and took good care of them. The sexual abuse, deeply repressed during my waking hours, was not a factor. In my mind, he didn't deserve what might happen if I told someone – what I was afraid would happen now that I had spilled my secret.

For the rest of the day, I avoided being alone with Candice. I hoped that she would forget about it or think it wasn't a big deal as long as I acted like it wasn't. I did my best to act normal in all of my classes, something that was easy considering how much practice I'd had doing that very thing, and by the end of the day I'd convinced myself that it was going to be okay. Candice wasn't going to say anything. I myself would never tell anyone ever again. Life would continue on as normal.

My fantasy only lasted until the next morning. Candice was waiting for me when I got off the bus. Grabbing me by the arm, she dragged me inside to a quiet corner of the gym, far away from all our other friends, saying, "Listen, we have to talk."

I wanted to resist, but I didn't want to draw attention to myself, so I went along. Feigning ignorance, I asked, "Why? What's wrong?"

"I talked to the school counselor about what you said…"

Cutting her off, I yelled angrily, "What!? Why would you do that?"

"I didn't tell him who I was talking about! I just told him that a friend had told me her dad was abusing her. I wanted to know what to do about it!"

"No, Candice," I said. "It's none of your business. You don't get to do anything about it. Just forget I told you!" I turned to stalk away, but she grabbed my arm.

"Listen, Emily," she said. "You don't have to let him do that. You have to tell someone. You have to!"

"No, I don't and I'm not going to."

Looking around, Candice saw that we were drawing attention. She pulled me closer to the corner and lowered her voice, saying, "But it's *wrong*. It's not okay for him to do that to you or to anyone."

My resolve began to crumble in the face of her certainty. I said, "I know it's wrong. But…what would happen to him? He'd go to jail or worse. I can't take that chance."

"Just think about it. Please?"

Looking at my friend's face, I saw real concern. Taking a deep breath, I said, "Okay, I'll think about it."

"Thank you," Candice said, pulling me into an uncharacteristic hug. I hugged her back, fighting tears.

A few hours later, in the free time after lunch, Candice told me, "Mrs. Wood is in our classroom waiting for you. Let's go talk to her."

Heart pounding, hands shaking, I didn't protest as I walked with Candice down the hallway toward our classroom. I wasn't quite sure how it had happened, but I knew I was going to tell my teacher. I couldn't know what was coming after I did it: visits with a social worker and police officer, writing my statement, my dad's arrest, working with the D.A. to prepare my testimony, a preliminary hearing and then a jury trial.

I didn't know then that my dad would admit to everything when questioned by the police, but would plead not guilty, anyway. Was it because he thought I would recant my story before the trial? Or because he honestly didn't believe he had done anything wrong? I still wonder.

I didn't know that my worst fears would soon be realized: my dad would be arrested, convicted of eight counts of molestation and one of injury to a minor child for a total sentence of 420 years plus life – a sentence that would end merely eight months after the trial, when he was murdered in his prison cell.

I didn't know the fear, guilt, and shame that lay in wait to shape every aspect of the next two decades of my life.

I couldn't know any of what was to come, but when I reached the door of the classroom where my teacher waited, I hesitated anyway.

Candice, determined enough for both of us, pulled the door open and ushered me inside.

A lifetime later

I lay across my bed, listening hard to the silence. It was one of those rare Saturdays that I had the house to myself: my husband and twelve-year-old son were away for the day doing father-son stuff; my daughter was spending the day with a friend. As a full-time college student and homeschooling parent, I was unaccustomed to having free time. I had no homework. No grading to do. Nothing. I was even less accustomed to enjoying said free time at home alone. Ordinarily I would have been ecstatic to find myself in such a state, but today the silence in my house was loud – too loud. Or maybe not loud enough. All I could hear were the thoughts in my head, and I would have given anything to drown them out. Helpless against them, however, I just stared at the ceiling, unable to focus except on the thing I had been successfully avoiding for weeks.

Alas, the busyness of life, always so faithful, had failed me in my moment of direst need.

Beside me on the bed were a notebook and a pen. Together with the quiet house, they should have been enough to accomplish the task I both dreaded and believed was necessary, but I still lacked one thing.

Courage.

The last six months had been particularly difficult, beginning with the sudden and unexpected death of my best friend. The loss had opened up wounds in my heart that I had long repressed, ignored, or pretended away. Grief, in its piercing, relentless fury, had stripped away every layer of protection that time and distance had provided. Every crutch with which I kept myself upright was broken and tossed aside. Every scab was ripped away to reveal the bleeding, gaping wounds beneath. To the outside world I looked the same as ever – eyes a little puffier, smile a little slower, but basically the same. Yet on the inside, I was broken.

I feared irreparably so.

But that made sense – the fear that I was irreparably broken – because after the loss of my friend, fear had come first. At first it was irrational: I would drive over a bridge and have a vision of my children drowning in the water below; the phone would ring and I would imagine the caller on the other end saying my husband was dead. The sudden loss of my friend had shaken my faith that everything would always be okay. I had begun to fear that it absolutely wouldn't be okay, perhaps ever again.

Over time, I began to experience fear in my relationships as well, particularly in my marriage. I had begun to believe that if my husband truly new me – really, deeply knew who I was on the inside – then he would leave me. This thought drifted in my subconscious, a constant companion: *He could never love me if he knew.* I never lingered long enough on the thoughts to consider what it was I feared he would find out. But love, I believed, was a choice. Given all the facts, withholding no information, would my husband of thirteen years really continue to choose to love me? Even if he knew it all?

No, I thought. Why would he? How could he?

I was broken, after all. So broken.

My fear, mixed with the all-consuming, unrelenting grief for my friend, brought with it anger and embarrassment. I hated how badly I'd handled my grief. *You should be over this by now*, a voice whispered. *You should be back to normal! Just be* normal*!!*

For six months, I had trudged through my inner turmoil in silence, doing my best to hide the war being waged in my mind. Not that I had grieved the loss of my friend in secret – oh, no. My grief had been so public, in fact, that I cringed remembering the countless church services I had sobbed through, and the ladies retreat where I cried non-stop for nearly 24 hours. My emotions were so much easier to control when I was alone, and as embarrassed as I was by my emotional displays, it was easy to withdraw. I stopped volunteering at church. I stopped calling my friends, and began attending only as few social gatherings as my husband would allow. My world shrank to school, home, and Sunday morning service. I was happy that way.

Or at least surviving.

But I couldn't continue as I was. My marriage, always so strong despite its unorthodox beginning, had begun to feel shaky. Uncertain. I had no doubt it was my fault. We were in no danger of divorce, but I knew that if I didn't address my issues, the shakiness would lead to a complete collapse. So, finally, I had sought out help in the form of Lynné, a friend and counselor from my church. Lynné had given me an assignment and was now waiting to see me again after its completion.

"I want you to write your story," Lynné had said. "From your earliest memories to the present. When you're done, we'll get together and talk through it."

"That sounds awful," I had said weakly, trying to pass it off as a joke.

"It's not easy," Lynné replied with a smile. "But worth it for the freedom at the end."

But I wasn't convinced. "I've told my story countless times," I said, thinking of the all the church retreats where I'd been a speaker. I had stood before many different groups of women and told my story: two years of molestation and rape by my father that ended a few months before my twelfth birthday, sexual activity beginning at age thirteen, marriage due to pregnancy at age seventeen, and years of struggle because I didn't understand the impact of being sexually abused. I was even *glad* to tell my story because it was one that too many women could relate to, a story that needed to be told so that every woman in the audience could silence the lie that said *I'm the only one*. Still, I didn't see the point of rehashing it all on paper.

"Two questions," Lynné said. "First, when you tell your story, do you ever leave anything out?"

Cautiously, I replied, "A few things."

"Because you're telling it for other people, right?"

"Right. There are some things those ladies don't need to know. Or *want* to know, for that matter."

"This time," Lynné said, "I want you to write your story for you. Don't leave anything out, no matter how painful or embarrassing. If it's the thing you never wanted to tell anyone in your whole life – write it down."

Seeing that I still wasn't convinced, she continued, "Sometimes we get hung up on things in our past without ever knowing how they've affected us. We form beliefs about ourselves without ever recognizing them for what they are: lies based on false information. But you're looking for the truth in your story. I think you'll find that it's not what you always thought."

"The truth," I said.

She smiled. "It sets you free."

Now, after weeks of avoiding it, I knew I couldn't put it off any longer. "God," I prayed aloud, "help me to find the truth."

Then with a deep breath, I put my pen to the page.

Memories flooded my mind so fast it was hard to get them all down. Details I hadn't thought about in years stood out in perfect clarity.

I wrote about the nights I was awakened by rape, when I screamed and cried for someone to save me but no one ever did – not my brothers, who were only children themselves, too scared and confused to intervene, and not my grandmother, who also lived in the apartment and was without excuse.

I wrote about the person who had started calling me a slut and a whore when I was ten or eleven years old, before anyone even knew I was being raped and molested. For all of my teenage years, right up until my marriage, if I ever did anything wrong, I was told it was because I was a slut and a whore. I had tried to prove the name-caller wrong for a while, but eventually I had unconsciously accepted that it must be true. I seemed to be a magnet for boys who knew I would give them what they wanted. It was as though they could just tell by looking at me who I was. What I had done. That "no" and "stop" weren't even in my vocabulary.

I wrote about that guy whose name I can't remember, whom I had consciously chosen to have sex with at sixteen simply because I knew if I did, he would never call me again. By then my pattern of sexual activity was well established; giving in was easier than saying no.

I wrote about all those nights when I was a child that I tried so desperately to stay awake. *If I stay awake he won't touch me,* I'd thought. *Just stay awake!* Yet sleep refused to be denied; I always fell eventually. Now as an adult, with no reason to stay awake and nothing to protect myself from, my body had finally figured out how to avoid falling asleep: insomnia. It felt like the ultimate betrayal. Sleep, as the most natural of the body's functions, should have been my friend. Instead it was my enemy. As a child, I'd been powerless against it. Twenty years later, I was powerless still.

As I wrote, I saw a picture of a little blond child in my mind. The girl cowered in a corner, the broken pieces of a glass figurine scattered before her. That figurine, she believed, had been her only chance to have something beautiful. *Her only chance.* But she had broken it.

Keeping it safe had been her only chance to *be good* – whatever that meant. But she had ruined it.

With mounting panic, the child waited now, terrified of being found out.

I realized that the little girl was who I'd always thought I was: a girl who had ruined my one chance to have something beautiful. Not because of the sexual abuse – by grace, I'd never once believed that had been my fault. But what came after…I had chosen those things. The boyfriends, the sex, the giving in – my choices, all of them.

Now, seeing my past clearly for the first time, I grieved for the girl who made those choices. That child had never stood a chance. She could not have chosen differently – not because she was inherently bad, not because she was a slut or a whore, but because she was *a child*.

Not a child who was broken, but a child with a broken foundation. Somehow, that made all the difference.

A few days later, after sharing my whole story first with Lynné and then my husband, I stood before an outdoor fire pit, the crumpled pages I had written gripped loosely in my hand. Just four pages, front and back, they held what had begun as my story, but had become like someone else's – the story of the girl that I had finally, *finally*, realized I wasn't anymore.

Not sparing the folded pages a single glance, I dropped them into the flames. As the paper caught, flared, and slowly turned black, I rolled my shoulders, marveling at the weight I no longer carried.

At the shame I no longer felt. At the lies I no longer believed.

This, I thought as I walked away. *This is what freedom feels like.*

●●●●●●●●●●●●●●●●●●●●●●●●●●●●●●●

Leah's Story

Leah was seventeen when it happened to her. She was surprised, actually, that it had never happened before. Eric, the on-again, off-again boyfriend she had had for the previous few years had threatened to force her to have sex with him many times. Since he had established a pattern of using violence against her to get his way early in the relationship, she had not doubted he would do it eventually, but he never followed through. He had used coercion instead. Manipulation. She had finally given in the night of the junior prom.

"So at least I knew what was happening," she would say later. "If I hadn't, maybe I would have fought harder."

By the spring of her senior year in high school, Leah and Eric were in an off-again stage. Her friend Courtney, who attended a different high school than she did, invited Leah to an after-prom party thrown by one of Courtney's classmates. Leah and Courtney had been friends since junior high, keeping up their friendship despite being in different schools, so the choice as to whether or not she would go to the party was an easy one: she told her parents she was staying the night with Courtney and off she went. When she arrived, the party was in full swing. Courtney was already there with her boyfriend, and Jess, the party's hostess, greeted Leah at the door with a cold beer and a welcoming smile.

The party was like something out of a movie, albeit a real-life portrayal of high-schoolers, not some sugary Disney depiction. The house, a two-storied, terraced affair in an affluent neighborhood, was bursting with teenagers and young twenty-somethings, most of them drunk, many of them high, everyone apparently having a good time. Leah, who accepted the beer Jess had offered her when she arrived, fit in seamlessly. Courtney, already happily tipsy, dragged Leah through the house, introducing her to more people than Leah could possibly remember.

One of the guys she met was Adam, Jess's older brother. With broad shoulders, dark hair, and impossibly blue eyes, Adam was gorgeous. For reasons Leah couldn't understand, Adam spent quite a bit of time flirting with her, which was as flattering to Leah as it was irritating to Courtney. As "the pretty one," Courtney was usually the one to get all of the attention from guys, while Leah was her stereotypical brunette sidekick. Chagrinned, Courtney pulled Leah into the bathroom to discuss it.

"I think he likes you," she admitted grudgingly. "But he's too old for you, *and* he's my friend's brother. It would be too weird."

Since Adam was twenty-two, Leah agreed that he was too old for her, if only because she knew it would be too much drama with her parents if she wanted to date him. Still, Courtney's attitude rankled. She had her own boyfriend, after all. Why was she jealous of Adam's attention to Leah? "He's not that much older," Leah told her. "And besides, what do you care if I date him?"

"I don't!" Courtney huffed. "It would just be weird, that's all."

At that moment, someone knocked on the bathroom door, bringing the conversation to an end.

Leah didn't drink anything besides the beer when she first arrived, so before long she was enlisted to drive the less-sober people to the Taco Bell a few blocks away for late night snacks. She made trip after trip, piling as many people as possible into her little yellow car. Once the trips started, she didn't see Adam much, but that was fine with her, despite what she'd told Courtney. Adam seemed nice enough, but he was cocky. Leah had had enough of that kind of guy with Eric, whom she hadn't seen in a few weeks, since the last time he'd slapped her. She wasn't looking to replace Eric with a guy who could be just like him, so she didn't mind not seeing him around.

But after the last trip, Adam met her at the door. He said, "I guess you're staying here tonight?"

Courtney had already told Leah she was planning to stay the night. Looking around, Leah saw that the party had really wound down. There were teenagers sprawled everywhere – on the furniture, in the floor, even on the kitchen table. She spotted Courtney, who beckoned her to follow her up the stairs. Leah knew she couldn't go home because her parents thought she was staying at Courtney's. She didn't really want to stay; being the lone sober person in a house full of drunks all night didn't sound like much fun. But not seeing any way out of it, she replied, "It looks like it."

"Want me to help you find a place to crash?" Adam asked.

'That's OK. I'm sleeping in the bedroom with Courtney," Leah replied, slipping away. She thought she felt Adam's eyes on her as she climbed the stairs, but when she looked back, she saw him talking to another girl. "He's not *that* interested," she mumbled to herself, partly relieved but strangely irritated. She found the bedroom she and Court-ney would be sleeping in. It had two twin beds pushed up against opposite walls. Courtney was already sitting on one of the beds in her pink camisole, pulling off her jeans. Her bra was on the floor beside the bed.

"Look!" she said excitedly when Leah walked in. "Jess let me borrow a pair of Adam's boxers to sleep in. How fun is that?!" she exclaimed as she pulled them on.

Leah just smiled, trying to hide her annoyance at the mention of Adam's name. She didn't really like him, didn't even want to talk to him, but had thought he liked her. Recognizing the irrationality behind her irritation and hating it, she decided to change the subject. "Will we have this room to ourselves?"

"I doubt it," Courtney said. "I thought we'd both sleep in this bed."

With a shrug, Leah crawled into bed beside her, wishing she had something more comfortable than her romper to sleep in, but unwilling to ask for something else. After they were settled, Courtney said, "I saw you talking to Adam downstairs. What were you guys talking about?"

"He just asked if I was staying the night," she replied. And then, wishing even while she was speaking that she would have kept her mouth shut, she said, "As soon as I came upstairs, he started flirting with another girl. I really don't think he likes me like that."

"Oh," Courtney said, trying and failing to sound sincerely disappointed for her friend. "He's been flirting with all of the girls here all night, even me when John's not around. Have you actually flirted back? Maybe he can't tell you like him."

I don't really like him, Leah thought, but she said, "You know I don't know how to flirt."

"Oh, come on, it's easy! Especially if you actually like the guy. You're not still hung up on Eric, are you?"

Courtney knew that Leah and Eric were broken up, but she didn't know how violent Eric had become. That was a secret Leah was trying to keep, knowing it would get blown all out of proportion if anyone knew. Besides, she was handling it, right? She had broken up with him, after all. She said, "No, I'm done with him. I just…"

But she was cut off when the door opened and Adam walked in. "There you are," he said with a smile. "I've been looking for you two. Just wanted to make sure you weren't sleeping on the floor somewhere."

Courtney gave Leah a sidelong glance and nudged her with her elbow, but Leah didn't say a word. Then Adam said to Courtney, "Where's your boyfriend? I thought he'd be up here with you."

"I don't know," she said, feigning unconcern. She propped herself up on her elbows so that the blanket slid down, uncovering her chest. "He's not *really* my boyfriend. We just hang out sometimes."

Leah almost laughed at how classically *Courtney* that was. Courtney and John had been together almost six months, but she wasn't beyond stretching the truth if it meant getting attention from another guy.

At that moment, John walked in. "Are you gonna sleep over there?" he slurred. Then, grinning stupidly as he fell onto the other bed, he said, "Don't you wanna sleep over here with me?"

Courtney seemed to instantly forget that she had been enjoying Adam's attention a second earlier. She jumped out of bed, breasts bouncing beneath her thin cami, and pranced across the room. "You know I do, baby," she said, giggling as she crawled in beside him.

As the sound of passionate kissing filled the room, Leah rolled her eyes and pulled the blanket up over head. It wasn't the first time she had been in a room where Courtney and one of her boyfriends were having sex, but that didn't make the situation easier to accept. In her head, she had just begun to repeat the mantra she employed whenever Courtney did something thoughtless – *Courtney is my friend and I love her, Courtney is my friend and I love her* – when she felt the bed dip. Pulling the covers down she saw Adam sitting next to her, smiling.

"Does your friend do this a lot?" he whispered.

Leah smiled, but again didn't reply. She didn't really want to encourage Adam to stick around, especially since, for all intents and purposes, she was now alone in the room. Feeling vulnerable, she tightened the blanket around her and looked away, hoping he would get the hint.

He didn't.

Standing up, Adam stripped off his jeans and climbed into bed beside her without ever saying a word.

"What...what are you doing?" she asked him.

"I just thought I'd get comfortable," he replied. "This is my room, after all."

Damn it, Courtney! she thought. *Why didn't you tell me whose room we were in?*

Trying not to display her mounting panic, Leah said, "I didn't know this was your room." She began to sit up, saying, "I'll just find somewhere else to sleep."

Adam threw his arm up, blocking her way off the bed. "No, it's fine," he said, "I don't mind if you sleep with me."

Feeling trapped, Leah lay back down. "Oh," she breathed, "I'll just...um...I'm pretty tired, so I'll just go to sleep then." She scooted against the wall, trying to get as far away as she could, but Adam was having none of it. He pressed in closer.

"Do you mind if I kiss you?" he asked.

"Um, I don't..." but he cut her off, pressing his mouth onto hers.

OK, she thought. *This is OK. He's just kissing me.* Then she felt his hand groping her waist, apparently trying to find a way under her romper. Giving up, he squeezed her breast before pulling her top down.

"I don't..." she started to say, but he pressed his mouth onto hers, cutting her off. Struggling, she pushed his face away from hers. "I don't want to do this," she said, louder than she intended.

The room was dead silent for a moment: no more kissing noises from the other bed, no more giggling. But the silence only lasted for a few seconds. Leah heard John say, "What is..." but Courtney shushed him with her furious whispers. Soon they began kissing and moaning again, more fervently than before.

Adam seemed not to notice any of it. "Sure, you do," he said.

"No, I really don't." Thinking fast, beginning to feel the futility of her situation, she said, "I don't have any protection or anything." But he was already pulling her romper off.

It was only then that she knew what was going to happen. *He's going to rape me,* she thought. For a very brief second she considered trying to fight him off, but her body seemed to freeze. *He wants me to fight. He wants me to fight,* was all she could think. So she didn't. She lay completely still while he pushed her panties to the side and forced himself into her.

She never made a sound.

When he was finished, he tried to kiss her again, but she turned her face away.

Smirking, he said, "So how was it?"

"I told you I didn't want to do that," she said loudly – loudly enough to leave no doubt that the others in the room heard her.

"Yeah," he replied smugly, as he settled himself onto the bed beside her, throwing a heavy arm and leg over her body. "But you did," he said.

And then he went to sleep.

What was left of the night passed slowly. Anytime Leah attempted to move, to extricate herself from his grasp, Adam used his weight to hold her still. It wasn't until daylight had begun to creep through the window between the two beds that Leah was able to make her escape. She fumbled around the bed as quietly as she could, trying to find her romper and her purse in the half-light. When she finally found them, she grasped them to her chest and rushed to the bathroom across the hall. Dropping her purse, she collapsed on the toilet, exhausted. But at the sudden tap on the door, Leah jumped up, heart pounding.

"Hey," Courtney whispered loudly from the other side of the door. "Can I come in? I've really got to pee."

Numbly, Leah unlocked the door. Courtney stumbled in and went straight for the toilet, saying, "God, I didn't get any sleep last night! I feel like shit this morning." She never once looked at Leah, but kept her gaze on the floor as if her head hurt too much to lift her eyes. She continued, "It was a fun party, though, huh? I'm glad you came." She launched into a story of something that happened the night before, telling it as though Leah hadn't been there and seen it firsthand. She laughed while she talked, neither noticing nor caring that Leah, shakily stepping into her romper, never once responded.

Finally dressed, Leah turned to Courtney, unsure of what to say. Seeing Adam's boxers pooled around Courtney's feet, knowing that Courtney knew exactly what had happened but was refusing to acknowledge it – it was too much. She turned away, but caught sight of herself in the mirror. Time froze as she stared at her face; Courtney's voice, still prattling away in the background, was muffled. Leah didn't know what she'd expected to see, but it wasn't this – this normal face, the same face she'd had the day before. She looked tired, with dark circles ringing her eyes, but otherwise exactly the same.

How can I be the same? she wondered.

Without a word, Leah walked out of the bathroom. Leaving the door open and Courtney squealing a protest from the toilet, she rushed down the stairs, out the door and to her car. She looked in the rearview once as she drove away, half expecting to see Adam behind her, smirking – and he *was* there. Perhaps not in the flesh, but he was there, nonetheless.

Five Years Later:

If there is one thing Leah understands, it's guilt.

She carries it with her at all times, its weight a constant reminder of what she's done. Her guilt is like a stone around her neck or, more accurately, like the stinking corpse of the girl she believes herself to be, strapped to her back every moment. It whispers to her, "If you had fought back, this wouldn't have happened. You could have stopped it, you could have struggled, but you didn't. *You didn't you didn't you didn't.*"

Her guilt is heavy – unbearably heavy – but impossible to set aside, impossible to leave behind. Not that she hasn't tried. She has laid it down a thousand times, even thrown it to the ground in fits of righteous rage, stomping on its face as her heart screamed *I DON'T DESERVE YOU!*

But she always takes it up again. Always. Because it is not just a part of her; it is who she is.

"Hello," her heart says. "My name is Leah, and I allowed myself to be raped."

Over the years, she has relived the rape countless times, always pinpointing the exact moment she decided to let him do it, when she thought, "I could fight back, but that's probably what he wants." In the fear of the moment, it didn't occur to her that he would get what he wanted either way.

And what would she get?

Self-loathing.

Anger.

Immeasurable loss.

Over the last five years, Leah has learned that there is so much more to rape than the event itself. The trauma of being raped, along with the trauma of enduring a long-term physically and emotionally abusive relationship, has continued to inform her present, despite both being firmly in her past. It has led her to drop a college class because of the muscular frame and commanding presence of the male professor. Even with the thirty other students who filled the class, her anxiety at being in the same room with him was uncontrollable, making it impossible for her to focus on anything but the need to get away. That same anxiety also determines which men she will date, so that she cannot form relationships with men who appear strong enough to overpower her.

Not that she has been hindered from dating. She has had plenty of relationships – if you could call them that. Because that's another thing she's learned about rape: it makes you appreciate, more than you ever knew you could, your opportunity to choose. So she *has* chosen: one long-term relationship, countless one-night stands with friends or strangers, even a series of trysts with a man old enough to be her father. She has made the choice to engage in sexual activity. She has *needed* to make the choice, to go into sex with eyes wide open and a mind that says *I choose this. I am in control.*

But that doesn't mean she uses her control well. Instead of choosing men with whom she can truly connect, she chooses the ones who lie to her, who cheat on her, who are emotionally distant or manipulative. She chooses men who treat her terribly – and why?

Because that is what she believes she deserves.

Shame.

It is her identifier. Shame says, "This is who you are: a girl who was raped because she chose not to fight back; a girl who went on to screw around with every halfway suitable man she met, including an old high school teacher, just because she could; a girl who will never be good enough for a decent man because no decent man would ever, *ever* love a girl like her."

If Leah is her guilt, how much more is she her shame.

Were you to see Leah today, you would never know who she is on the inside. You would see a pretty girl, smart, dedicated to her school work. You would see a sassy twenty-two-year-old with countless cute dresses and an inexplicable abhorrence for jeans, who always looks adorable even when she doesn't because she is *just that loveable*. You would not lay eyes on her without smiling or think of her without being grateful she is your friend.

You would never know the secrets she carries. You would only see what she wants everyone to see: a normal girl. Until Leah and I sat down together so she could tell me her story, she, like every sexual abuse and assault survivor, believed she was the only one. Until I told her my story, she had always believed the guilt, shame, anxiety, and even her driving need to *choose* were personal weaknesses rather than normal, expected responses to being raped. She had been judging herself by an impossible standard, fully believing that her life should fit the shape of the "normal girl" she wanted everyone to believe she was. She didn't know – couldn't have known – the perfect incredulity of a sexually-traumatized girl making the same informed choices as one who has never been sexually assaulted. Holding herself to that standard had kept her in a perpetual cycle of self-destruction that only compounded her shame.

And then compounded it again and again.

The last time I saw Leah, she looked the same as always – cute, sassy, opinionated – but she was different, too. She was enrolled in a class with the same professor who had sent her into a panic the year before. Her boyfriend, broad and muscular and standing a foot and half taller than her, was unlike any man she had ever dated. While she undoubtedly has a long way to go, she's made great strides on her journey toward healing, strides she couldn't have made without learning the truth about sexual trauma. Nor would she have made such strides without confronting *her* truth. By telling her story, she brought the beliefs she held in secret into the light. Uncovered and unmasked, they lost their power. She was finally able to throw them off – her guilt and shame – and walk away, unburdened.

She has begun to live in the freedom she never dared hope for: the freedom to love herself, even *like* herself, just as she is, while allowing herself the time and space to heal. To grow.

It is truly a beautiful thing to see.

Part II

A Change of Perspective

L ike most sexual abuse survivors, I participated in silence for years after my abuse ended. Conversely, however, my silence was private rather than public. As a retreat speaker and small group leader, there was a time I felt that half my church had heard my story. My pastors, other church leaders, my friends and ladies I mentored – all of them had heard the details. The only person who hadn't heard it was the one who suffered the effects of it every day, yet understood none of it: my husband.

For the first thirteen years of our marriage, when I refused to make love nine times out of ten, he had no idea that it was because I couldn't bear to feel pushed or pressured. He didn't know that lying beside him every night made sex feel like something I *had* to do, like I was obligated, and that both my body and mind rebelled against the feeling. He didn't know that enjoying myself during foreplay and intercourse felt wrong, shameful. He didn't know that I wanted him as much as he wanted me, but I was compelled by forces I didn't understand to refuse, resist, and sometimes even run away.

He knew only what my actions seemed to tell him: that I didn't really love him, that he wasn't enough for me, that I wasn't happy in our marriage.

My mom had told him before we were married that I had been sexually abused, but that conversation was the first and last time my abuse experience was spoken of in his presence. I had kept every moment of my journey a secret from him. He had never heard the truth of my sexual history, didn't understand why sex was impossible for me to initiate and nearly as difficult for me to enjoy. He didn't know the depth of shame that dictated my self-worth.

Then came the night I had to tell him the whole truth. It was the same day I had met with Lynné a second time, the day I had read to her my completed story. She'd cried with me, held my hand, prayed over me, and encouraged me to take the final step: reading the story to my husband. The longer I hid it, she told me, the more power it would have, but sharing it with him, allowing myself to be fully known by him, would open the door for intimacy between us like we'd never known. I wanted that intimacy, knew our marriage needed it desperately, but my old fears lingered. What would he think of me? Would he still love me if he knew it all?

For the first time in over twenty years, however, my desire for freedom was stronger than my fear. That night after we put the kids in bed, I told him everything. The abuse. My body's traitorous reaction to it and what I'd always believed that reaction said about me. My complete sexual history. My shame at how long the abuse had been controlling my life.

How can I describe his response? He was shaken by what he heard. Grieved. Even brokenhearted.

But he was not disgusted.

He was not repulsed.

He did not reject me as my shame had convinced me he would. Instead, his heart broke for the little girl I had been and in many ways still was. He grieved over the years of intimacy we had lost in our marriage – a loss he believed wasn't due to my secrets, but rather to his own blindness.

He said, "I knew that you'd been abused, but I just thought it didn't affect you."

Oh, silence, you dirty liar.

You did that.

My husband's words, so heartfelt, were as much a surprise to me as my story had been to him. The root of my struggles had always seemed so obvious to me that I never considered it might not be obvious to him as well. As a result, I had spent a great deal of our marriage believing that he *did* know that my abuse history is what made sexual intimacy so difficult for me, but that he just didn't care. The more I resisted, the more he pushed, leaving me to believe that he felt his needs were simply more important than my own. He was never forceful, only insistent, but it was enough to reinforce my belief that I *shouldn't* be struggling because of my abuse. I felt I must be a disappointment to him. A failure.

Understanding the truth from his perspective cast the painful incidents of our past in an entirely different light. His words brought healing to my heart, just as my total honesty had brought healing to his.

Silence is powerful, but the truth is more so.

That conversation would later become a chief catalyst for this book. It was the reason I realized how truly deceptive silence can be. Knowing from experience that an abuse survivor is vulnerable to deception in her beliefs about herself and about the lifelong impact of sexual abuse, I had never considered how vulnerable non-survivors are to the same lies. Just as the survivor's view of herself is distorted by her experience, the non-survivor's view of her is distorted as well. A person who has not been sexually abused has no way to understand an abuse survivor's pain and her response to it. The non-survivor can only judge the survivor's actions and motivations by the standard of someone who is not carrying the weight of unresolved sexual trauma. In my story, that meant my husband mistaking my sexual dysfunction for willful obstinacy and dissatisfaction. What might it look like for others?

It might look like seeing a promiscuous young woman and immediately thinking *slut,* but never *victim.*

Or like seeing an adult woman bound by depression, anxiety, or some other form of mental illness and thinking *crazy,* but never *surviving.*

It's the same judgment survivors turn on themselves, a standard list of *shoulds* and *shouldn'ts.* Fifteen-year-old girls should not be drinking alcohol, using drugs, self-harming, or engaging in sexual activity. When we see one who does, we find it easy to point fingers, shake our heads, and lament the downward spiral of today's youth. We rarely consider her motivations for doing the things she does, and if we do, the expected culprits are usually blamed: permissive parenting, sex in the media, attention seeking.

But mostly, we fault the girl.

And perhaps some of those things, or many others, *are* to blame. Maybe her parents or caregivers *are* permissive, or *are* weak disciplinarians. Maybe she has been conditioned through the media to believe that sexual activity and self-harm are fashionable.

But maybe – just maybe – she's walking out the perfectly normal response to sexual trauma. Maybe an early introduction to sexual activity led her to promiscuity. Maybe alcohol, drugs, and self-harm are the tools she uses to repress her shame. Maybe she's not at all who we think she is, or even who *she* thinks she is.

Maybe she is only the reflection of her abuse experience: Broken. Distorted. Unheard.

And the cycle continues. Scowling from afar, we make our judgements, never even questioning if we're right, while she remains silent. Her heart, trapped and tortured by shame and guilt, never gets the chance to heal.

And the cycle continues.

The Role of Protectors

As noted at the beginning of the third chapter, we all have beliefs about child sexual abuse that impact the way we think and interact with the world. Our beliefs shape the way we see survivors, determining whether we hear or refuse to hear their stories. They also shape our expectations of the survivor's healing process. Our beliefs have the capacity to hurt or to help the survivors in our lives, but for no other group are those beliefs as potentially devastating as they are for parents and caregivers.

In my journey from sexual abuse victim to advocate, I've encountered adults with all kinds of philosophies regarding abuse prevention. There was the Hopeful parent, who believed that her abuser had "changed" and wouldn't molest or rape another child if given the chance. This particular mother allowed her child to spend time with her abuser because she had convinced herself it was safe to do so. Thankfully, she changed her mind before her daughter suffered as she had, and has since limited the carefully supervised time her daughter spends in the man's presence.

Then there was the Accepter, who was sexually abused by nearly every man in her life when she was a child: her father, uncles, and grandfather. Though she never had any children of her own, she had nieces who she knew were being abused by those same men. However, it never occurred to her to speak up, to protect them from the abuse, just as it had never occurred to her to speak up when she was the victim. I cannot say whether she allowed her family members to continue being abused in order to protect the abusers or because she truly believed sexual abuse is normal, but her actions spoke clearly her beliefs: sexual abuse must be endured, not prevented. She has helped perpetuate a cycle of abuse that may continue for generations if her nieces – or their daughters, or the daughters after them – carry on with the same deceptions passed down to them by their should-be protectors.

Then of course there are the Oblivious parents and caregivers, who do not protect their children simply because they don't realize that sexual abuse is an actual risk. The Adamant parent, who refuses to believe that anyone they know could possibly molest a child. And also, the Steadfastly Blind parent, for whom the truth is so painful that they prefer to live in denial, regardless of the consequences for the children in their care. I've also encountered parents who understand that sexual abuse is a real risk, but who refuse to take practical steps to protect their children out of the belief that doing so means being overly protective or fearful. They say, "I don't want to live in fear of my child being molested. What kind of life would that be for them?"

My response is this: as parents, we protect our children from threats to their health and safety all the time. We make them wear a seat belt in the car not because we're living in fear, but because we love them too much to senselessly expose them to the potential dangers of a car accident. We teach them to wash their hands after using the bathroom and before they eat, not because we're living in fear of germs, but because we love them too much to allow them to become sick through preventable illness. It's the same reason we establish rules regarding the internet and social media. We're not living in fear of unsafe relationships forming online; we're just cognizant of the risks, and not we're willing to take any chances with our children's health and safety.

All of these protective decisions, and so many others, are based on the belief that our children are valuable. We make them because we have embraced our responsibility to do our best to protect our kids from harm and to prepare them to protect themselves when they are old enough to do so. Why, then, should protecting them from sexual abuse be any different?

Understandably, the very idea of someone molesting our child is unthinkable. So unthinkable, in fact, that the notion of taking practical steps to teach them about sexual abuse prevention can feel like participating in the defilement of their innocence. We think: *why bring up a subject that will surely never affect them anyway?* Besides, we naturally assume that our kids know without being told that it's okay to speak up if someone molests them. We parent as though they just *know* that they don't have to submit to sexual abuse. We rarely – I'd go so far as to say never – consider the confusion and fear a child is certain to feel if their abuser is someone they trust, as it is over 90% of the time[7]. We think they understand that sexual abuse is wrong, that they are victims of a crime, and that it's okay to speak up without ever being taught to do so.

But the truth is, they don't.

Children believe what they are told, and the abusers are the ones taking advantage of that fact. Sexually abused children are often told that the abuse is their fault, that they or their loved ones will be harmed if they tell, or that no one would believe them. Because they never hear or experience a different truth, abused kids can only build their beliefs about the abuse out of the lies of their abusers. They internalize those lies until they become truth: *This is my fault. He'll hurt me if I tell. No one would believe me anyway.*

Other abusers take advantage of the love and trust of the child. When a child loves their abuser, they feel responsible for protecting the abuser from the consequences of his or her actions. Telling feels like a betrayal. The child believes that telling would destroy their family – and whose fault would that be?

Sadly, from the child's perspective, it would be their own.

So, kids don't tell, plain and simple.

As a result, child molesters and rapists can feel confident that they won't be discovered. Statistically, only five in one hundred sexually abused children will ever tell an authority

So, kids don't tell, plain and simple.

only five in one hundred sexually abused children will ever tell

figure of their abuse[5]. Of those few cases, only a miniscule number of abusers will be prosecuted. The rest of them – men and women who look like everyone else, whom you would never identify as pedophiles or child molesters – carry out their abuse in relative safety, their crimes protected by their victims' silence.

Parents and caregivers, then, play a vital, irreplaceable role in protecting kids from abuse. No one has more insight, authority, and responsibility to speak into a child's life than their mom or dad – and if they don't, who will?

Sometimes – far too often – the answer is "no one."

Jill's Story

Sitting alone at the kitchen table, 14-year-old Jill watched in silence as her younger sister, Allie, moved from room to room, shoving her belongings into a large black trash bag. From the living room Jill could hear her mother, Bea, talking with the social workers who'd brought Allie by the house.

"Please," her mother said. "At least tell me where you're taking her."

The social worker replied, "I'm sorry, ma'am. I know you're concerned, but we can only tell you she'll be safe and taken care of."

As her mother continued to plead, Jill thought, *Any second now they'll come in here and ask me. What will I say? What will I say?*

It was a question she'd been asking herself all day. That morning she'd heard whispers in the school office about a girl in the junior high who had come to school covered in bruises. She'd known immediately it was Allie. Their father had come home stumbling drunk and angry the night before. Jill had recognized the signs the same second he walked in the house and had quietly escaped to her room, but Allie, engrossed in a T.V. show, hadn't even looked up. Just that small amount of perceived disrespect was enough to set their dad off when he was in one of his rages, and Jill had cringed behind her bedroom door as he started yelling. From the sound of it, the beating had been one of the worst.

"Please," she'd breathed after it was over, when the only sounds in the house were her sister's sobs and her father's footsteps in the hall, "please just go to bed. Please just go to bed."

But he hadn't. He'd come to her room instead.

The next morning Jill and Allie hadn't spoken a word to each other as they'd gotten ready for school. Their mother, just getting home from her night shift at the nursing home, had barely said anything to them either. Only to Allie, she said, "It's a little cool outside for that t-shirt. Why don't you go put a sweater on."

She either hadn't noticed that Allie had only put on a zip-up sweat-shirt over her t-shirt or she had thought, like Jill did, that Allie had never intended to wear the t-shirt to school without something over it, anyway. She and Allie never wore short-sleeved shirts to school. They always had bruises to hide. Why would today have been different?

Now, a mere nine hours later, their house was full of social work-ers and any second they were going to come into the kitchen and talk to Jill. They would ask her if her dad ever hit her or abused her. They would tell her she could be honest and promise to keep her safe. In her mind, as she practiced what she would say, she kept her story as short as possible: *He beats us with an extension cord when he's angry. Afterward, if mom's not home, he comes into my room and makes me have sex with him.*

"I'll tell them," she whispered to the empty kitchen. "If they ask me, I'll tell them."

But soon Allie came into the kitchen, bulging trash bag in hand. She didn't look at Jill or say a word to her, just walked straight through to the living room. Then Jill heard one of the social workers say, "Are you all ready to go?"

She didn't hear Allie's reply, just her mother crying as the door closed.

Then they were gone.

Jill's best friend was her next-door neighbor, Michelle. Michelle, whose parents had died when she was very young, was being raised by her grandparents. Jill, whose parents were alive but were barely parents at all, could relate to the loss Michelle felt. At eleven, Michelle was a few years younger than Jill, and having never known anything different and having never been told not to tell, one day she calmly asked, "Can

I stay the night at your house tonight? Grandpa's been looking at me weird all day. I don't really want to go home."

Jill felt like her heart stopped for a second before beating wildly. Slowly, cautiously, she asked, "What do you mean 'looking at you weird'?"

"You know, like he's definitely gonna want to do it tonight."

Forcing herself to match Michelle's casual tone, she said, "Your grandpa has sex with you?"

"Yeah," Michelle said with a frown. "I hate it, but he won't stop. Sometimes I just want to get away, that's why I want to stay at your house."

"My house isn't much different," Jill said.

"Your dad?" Michelle asked, sounding wise and understanding beyond her years.

Taking slow breaths, trying to pretend that it wasn't as awful as it really was, Jill said only, "Yeah."

The girls were quiet for a few moments before Michelle changed the subject. Neither of them ever brought it up in conversation again, but it became a frequent topic of the notes the two passed back and forth every day. Michelle began writing to Jill about the times her grandfather came into her room at night, explaining what he did to her or asked her to do as though it was completely normal. Jill, knowing perfectly well that it wasn't normal, but relieved to finally have someone to talk to about it, did the same. She told Michelle about how it started, the way her father would tell her to lie down on the couch in front of him to watch television. He'd pull a blanket over them and slowly inch her pants down. It happened nearly every day at first, even while her mother was home. He'd start molesting her while Bea was in the kitchen or another room and if she came into the living room, he'd just hold still until she left again, knowing she kept herself too busy to stay for long. Later he started making Jill stay home while Bea and Allie went to the grocery store or to run errands on weekends so he could take her to the bedroom – or the kitchen or bathroom or laundry room – to have sex with her. Then of course there were the nights Bea worked. He was never violent with her during those times like he was when he was angry. In fact, he was the opposite, whispering "I love you" over and over as if that excused what he did.

By the time Allie was taken away, Jill had been a victim of rape for years, and Michelle was the only one she had ever told about it. The notes they passed spared no detail. Finally able to talk about what they went through, both girls took full advantage of having someone who understood.

A few weeks after Allie went to foster care, Jill came in the back door after school one day to find her mother in the laundry room, a creased piece of paper in her hand and a look of horror in her eyes. Pale-faced and shaking, she looked up at Jill when she walked in. "Did you write this?" she demanded.

Jill, recognizing the page as the note she had written but never delivered to Michelle the day before, was suddenly terrified. Shaking her head emphatically, she said, "No."

"But you don't even know what it is," Bea said, shoving the note into Jill's hand. "Look at it! Did you write it?"

Jill looked down at the page, her eyes alighting immediately on the first paragraph. It read, "Since my sister's been gone, he's stopped wanting to have sex. I guess the court stuff scared him. He still makes me do other stuff, though." The rest of the note explained what had happened a few nights before, when Bea had left Jill at the apartment her dad was living in since the court had ordered him to move out of their house.

"No," she said again, "my friend wrote it."

Bea let out the breath she was holding. "That poor girl," she said. "But don't you bring something like that into this house again. It's disgusting." Then she walked away, leaving Jill alone in the laundry room, staring down at her handwriting.

At her story.

At her name signed on the bottom.

When the bell rang signaling the end of English class, Jill wondered how she was able to hear it over the sound of her own pounding heart. It was Monday, the day she would turn in the poetry packet she'd been working on for weeks, and she was nervous – more than nervous. Terrified. The assignment required students to write a poem from each of several different genres. For the most part, the topic of each of Jill's poems was typical for a high school English class: nature and homework and lost love – even though, at seventeen, as a junior in high school, she'd never had a boyfriend nor ever wanted one. But it's what everyone else was writing about, so why not? Writing those poems had been fun and a little challenging at times, but they hadn't required anything of her heart. Except for one.

The last poem in the packet had been on her mind from the start, but she'd fought against it. Ignoring the lines that formed in her mind, she'd refused to put them on paper. She demanded their silence, commanded them to bend to her will, but they hadn't. The poem, it seemed, was determined to write itself, and in the end, she chose to stop denying it. When she sat down to write she did so without stopping, without editing, without ever even reading it again. She scribbled the lines on notebook paper, tucked the page in the back of the folder, and never looked at it.

Now the time had come to turn the packet in, to drop the folder containing her life in a poem on her teacher's desk, and then traipse out of the classroom as though carefree. Feeling as though every eye in the room was turned toward her, she hoisted her backpack over her shoulder, grabbed the folder, and joined the line of students heading toward the front of the room. At her teacher's desk, she hesitated a second too long and was jostled when another student reached around her to put his folder in the basket. Hers fell out of her hand, landed perfectly on top of all the others, and she was swept out the door. Her fear rang like a fire alarm in her head, *Go back! Go back! Go back!* But, afraid like always of drawing attention to herself, she followed the crowd down the hall. From the outside, she looked like a typical teenage girl in a rush to get from class to softball practice without being late. On the inside, she felt partly like a criminal committing a heinous crime and partly like a drowning victim being pulled from the ocean.

It's done, she thought. *Now I wait.*

The next week passed the same as always. Her sister had returned from foster care about six months before, after claiming to have made up the allegations of abuse. Her father, cleared of all suspicion, had returned home as well. He was still violent when he was angry. When he wasn't angry, he still said "I love you" to each of them a hundred times a day. Only one thing had changed: he hadn't made Jill have sex with him since Allie told her story a year before. He still made her do other things when he caught her home alone, things that left Jill feeling confused and ashamed.

Finally, though, she had found a way to fight back: she simply never went home. She'd become active in sports that kept her at practice until dinner, then went to work bagging groceries until nine. By the time she got home each night, her mom, who had begun working a day shift, was home and it was time for bed. She didn't use the bathroom or shower when her father was home, didn't go into the laundry room or even her own bedroom until he had gone to bed himself. Sometimes he still snuck into her room at night, but only a few times a month.

Just one more year until graduation. Then she'd be gone – or so she had always planned. Now, after writing the poem and turning it in, her life could change any day. After reading the poem, her teacher would surely ask her about it, and she would finally be able to tell someone. The idea of it terrified her, but at the same time she felt the steel in her spine. She was ready. This time she would do it.

Every day after turning in the poem, she watched her English teacher closely. She walked into class breathless and nervous and walked out just the same, sure that he would stop her and demand she tell him the truth. She played out the scenario in her mind a thousand times: her teacher's concerned eyes, the walk to the principal's office to call the police. As each day passed she knew it would happen *today.*

But it didn't.

On Friday their graded assignments were returned. Flipping through the pages in disbelief, she came to the last poem, a full page of free verse called "Daddy Don't Hurt Me." It was about a little girl whose dad came into her bed at night. The girl in the poem cried silently as he removed her clothes and did what he did, telling her over and over, "Don't open your eyes, just keep them closed."

Next to the title, in red ink, were the words, "I hope this isn't about you."

Jill stared at the words, not trusting her eyes. She saw them blur and swim. Saw them settle back into place.

I hope this isn't about you.

The letters, scratched sharply onto the page, were hurried, trampling one another.

I hopethisisn't
aboutyou.

For a moment, she felt caught in the tight places between them. They pressed against her like a vice, constricting her movement, making it impossible to breathe. She tried to push them back, to force them aside, but they collapsed around her, sharp limbs clanging together. Their cacophony filled her ears. A death knell.

Slowly, Jill closed the folder. She did not look at her teacher as she left the classroom. Didn't look at him again for the rest of the school year, or at any of her teachers the year after that. She went to school, played sports, sang in the choir. She went to work, bagged groceries, stocked shelves. She hung out with her friends, their parents always commenting on what a pretty smile she had.

"You're always smiling," she heard again and again. "You're such a happy girl."

Just one more year, she thought.

Then, *Just a few more months.*

And finally, *Only one more day.*

She found a house to rent with a friend and moved out the day after graduation. Her father never said he loved her again.

They were words she could not miss.

Some day she would find people who *heard* her, who loved her in spite of the choices she made as she struggled to overcome her past. She would marry a man who *saw* her, who had prayed every day for a year that she would see him too. She would grow in relationship with the God of healing, who would take her damaged places and make them new.

Children, a career, a life – they were all coming.

Eventually.

But from April of her junior year until May of the next, she remained as she had been since childhood. Her teacher's words echoed in her mind every time her father told her, "Don't open your eyes. Just keep them closed."

I hope this isn't about you.

But it is, her heart cried – to her teacher, to her mother, to the entire world.

You just refuse to see it.

The Cost of Silence

A few years ago I walked into church a few minutes after praise and worship started, slid into one of the back rows, and found myself next to a woman I'd never met. Her hair was disheveled, her jeans torn, and her too-large t-shirt looked as though she'd slept in it – which I later found out she had, because, despite the fact that she'd overslept, she'd been so determined to come to church that day she'd run out of the house after doing nothing more than throwing on the first pair of jeans she could find. I spent some time talking with her after the service was over and found out quite a bit about her. Her name was Brook. She was married with two children, but her husband, Steve, didn't come to church. She'd recently moved to town and decided it was a good time to get her kids, seven-year-old Anna and four-year-old Nick, into church. Both she and Steve were unemployed, but they were both looking for jobs.

Over the next few weeks, we became friends. We sat together at church, she attended my small group, and our families spent some time together socially so that we could get to know her husband, Steve. Within a few months, he began attending church as well. He joined my husband's small group and both Steve and Brook attended the next Encounter retreat. They found jobs, though neither ever stayed at the same one for long, and they eventually purchased their first home.

From the outside, it looked as though they were moving in a good direction. However, over the course of our friendship it had become clear that they were being careful to conceal certain parts of their lives from us. I had learned to notice patterns in the way Brook talked that indicated what was true and what wasn't, and sometimes I was amazed at how brazen her lies could be. For example, one day she called to ask that I pray for Steve, who had been arrested on a burglary charge. She assured me that he could not have done it, as they were in a city a few hours away at the time, and I prayed right then that the truth would be revealed and true justice served.

And it was. Steve confessed, admitted to being high on methamphetamines at the time of the burglary, and was sentenced to probation as well as drug and alcohol counseling.

Though we learned not to take anything they told us at face value, we believed that they were growing and maturing. We believed they were trying to break out of the cycles of poverty they'd both been raised in, and perhaps they were. But then the day came, about five years after we first met, when I walked into church to find Brook sitting alone, crying. She said, "I found out on Friday that Steve has been having sex with Anna for a long time. She told a counselor at school and they called the police and the Department of Human Services and then me – and I just can't believe it," she ended on a sob. Over the next few minutes, the story came out in bits and pieces, many of which never made much sense. She told me that Anna, now twelve, had said she and Steve's relationship "had been sexual" for about a year – a telling turn of phrase, as Brook never used the words "rape" or "abuse," only calling what had happened between Steve and Anna "sex." She told me that Steve had been arrested, but couldn't be released on bail unless someone claimed responsibility for him. She said that she had to be that person, but since he was under suspicion for child abuse, they wouldn't allow her kids to go home with the two of them. As a result, she'd had to sign over custody of all three children to her mother.

Brook told me that she'd asked Steve that same day if Anna's story was true and he'd said no. She hadn't believed him, so the next morning she told him the investigators had called with DNA evidence from a rape kit that proved he had had sex with Anna. Steve confessed to her then, and after a huge fight, she'd forced him to leave. When she left for church that morning, she'd found him sleeping on the couch, but she hadn't talked to him.

"Now I have to go home and make him leave for good," she told me. "If he won't, I'll pack my stuff and go to mom's."

I called and texted her multiple times over the next couple of days, but I didn't hear much back at first. All she would tell me is that she was okay and they were both staying in the house until they could figure something else out. By mid-week, however, I received a call from her that I will never forget. She said, "Steve told me how Anna seduced him. He didn't want to do anything with her, but one day when they were home alone, she grabbed him and started giving him oral sex. She pushed him to have sex with her, and he eventually gave in."

For the next few minutes, she filled my stunned silence with more excuses and justifications, all of which laid the blame for the abuse solely on Anna, but I could only think one thing: when the abuse began, Anna had only been eleven.

Brook truly, sincerely believed her daughter had been responsible for seducing a thirty-year-old man.

How does that kind of deception even happen?

The answer, unfortunately, is simple: silence.

I had known for years that Brook had been sexually abused as a child by a few different men. She'd told her mother about the first one, but her mother had slapped her, called her a liar, and told her if it *had* happened, then it had been her fault. Every one of her abusers had always told her the same thing: she'd asked for it.

She'd wanted it.

It was her fault.

Brook had shared her experiences with me pretty early in our friendship, and I always believed we were of the same mind: sexual abuse is never the child's fault, and parents should protect their children no matter

sexual abuse is never the child's fault

the cost. I believed, foolishly, that her ability to speak easily about her experience meant she was healed – or at least healing. I believed she had rightfully attributed the responsibility of her abuse to her abuser, and that she recognized her mother's refusal to believe and protect her was wrong.

I never asked Brook what she really believed about her abuse experience. I don't know that it would have done any good if I had. Until faced with abuse in her own family, I doubt she even knew what she believed. She had spent years being lied to by the abusers in her life, and no one ever told her that what they said wasn't true. Not her mother, who undeniably failed her. Not society, whose silence on the subject was absolute. Not anyone else, because after telling her mother that one time, she vowed to never tell anyone again. By adulthood, her beliefs were a part of her reality: men don't want to have sex with children; they just do it because the child asks for it.

Even her own child.

The last I saw Anna, she was seventeen and had two children with two different fathers. I can't help but wonder what kind of mother she'll be. Will she break the cycle of abuse in her family, or will she follow the patterns of those who raised her? Will her son grow up understanding the respect and honor due another human person, or will he believe that he can take whatever he wants without responsibility? Will her daughter grow up understanding her intrinsic worth and value, or will she believe she is only as valuable as the object of someone's perverse sexual desire?

Statistically, the latter is true on all counts.

Somehow the patterns and generational cycles of abuse, drugs, and poverty can make it easy to write Brook and Anna's story off as an exception. After all, their family wouldn't classify as "normal" middle-class America, right? Instead, they fall neatly under the label of "those people," allowing us to be smugly comfortable in our assurance that no one we know would ever fall prey to the same deceptions that Brook did.

But is that true?

The Accepter I mentioned in the beginning of the previous chapter is the product of a squarely middle-class home. Her father, uncles, and grandfather are all upstanding businessmen of good repute in their community. No drugs, no alcohol, no poverty, yet extreme sexual abuse. Extreme deceptive beliefs on the part of the victim. Because sexual abuse is not a respecter of persons, no abuse survivor is insulated from that kind of deception. Sexual abuse doesn't care how stable a victim's home looks on the outside, how affluent her family is, or how bright her prospects. Its lies are not dependent on her socio-economic status, but only on her experience. If her experience tells her that that being raped was her fault, and she's never told anything different, then that is what she believes. Perhaps she'll come to understand the truth before her own children become victims.

But perhaps, like Brook, she will not.

Thankfully, not every sexual abuse survivor will fail to protect their children from sexual abuse. Many will go on to make healthy parenting choices that reflect wisdom, forethought, and awareness. Many will be open about their experience at appropriate times so that the child is aware of what to do if someone tries to molest them. But many others will refuse to acknowledge even the possibility of their child being sexually abused. The memory of their own trauma triggers emotions too difficult to confront, making it impossible to consider that their children may experience something similar. Others will simply believe that sexual abuse is a fact of life, and still others, such as the mother we saw in Jill's story, will choose blindness and denial in order to protect themselves from a heartbreaking truth. Regardless of the root of the belief, the result is too often the same: children are left vulnerable, cycles of abuse repeat, and a new generation of abuse victims begins.

The Simple Truth

While parents who are survivors of sexual abuse make parenting decisions based on their experience, parents who were never sexually abused do the same out of their naivete. That may mean they simply lack awareness of the probability of their child being sexually abused. It may mean they've heard the statistics but don't really believe that sexual abuse is a legitimate threat to their families. Perhaps they believe sexual abuse only happens to "those people," or is only perpetrated by weirdos in parks or on the internet.

The truth, however, is staggering: if you are reading this, you know a child who is being sexually abused.

You also likely know an abuser.

It's really that simple.

Yet, for the most part, both those who are survivors and those never experienced sexual trauma exchange the truth of sexual abuse for a number of comforting myths. Predicated on what we *want* to believe, these myths shape our parenting decisions and put our children at risk of being abused more than anything else.

FACTS VS MYTHS

MYTH: Child sexual abuse is a "lower class" problem.
FACT: Sexual abuse statistics are the same across all socio-economic, racial, religious, and ethnic lines[3]. We are all "those people."

MYTH: Child sexual abuse isn't really that common.

FACT: Though statistics vary between sources, the generally accepted statistic regarding sexual abuse is 1 in 4 girls and 1 in 6 boys. There are 46 million adult abuse survivors and nearly a million substantiated reports of sexual abuse every year[3], which says nothing of the number of children whose sexual abuse is never reported.

MYTH: Sexual abuse is only perpetrated by pedophiles.

FACT: While the majority of child molesters could be diagnosed with the disorder pedophilia, not all fit the criteria. According to the Child Molestation Research and Prevention Institute, child molesters also fall into one of three other categories[4].

1. Sexually curious children or teens who experiment with younger children (though not all adolescent perpetrators fall into this category).
2. Those with an untreated medical or mental condition, severe intellectual disability, or psychosis.
3. Those with an anti-social personality disorder. Such disorders can cause a person to appear social and even charming, but inside they believe society's rules don't apply to them. They lack feelings for others, believing that everyone, even children, exist to be used.

MYTH: If we teach our kids about "stranger danger," they will be safe from sexual abuse.

FACT: More than 90% of sexually abused children are victimized by people they know, love, and trust. Common perpetrators are parents, grandparents, aunts, uncles, cousins, friends, and babysitters[7].

In order for a perpetrator to successfully carry out long-term abuse, he or she must have regular access to the child – not just for the abuse itself, but also for the "grooming" process, which requires a strong relationship with the child and family. Grooming is the method an abuser uses to gain the child's trust. An adult who is intentionally grooming a child to accept abuse may show special interest in the child, giving the child extra attention, taking interest in the child's activities and hobbies, or giving the child gifts[3]. He or she may become the child's friend or confidant by encouraging the child to divulge secrets and allowing them to do things the parents wouldn't.

My father, for example, bought me cigarettes and allowed me to smoke, despite my young age. He also allowed me to hang out with my friends unsupervised (something that never happened when I was home with my mom), and even allowed me to spend time with older boys who had no business hanging around an eleven-year-old girl, thereby guaranteeing that I would be exposed to sexually explicit conversations from multiple sources. He couched his excessive permissiveness in kindness, establishing himself as the "fun" parent and ensuring that I would want to spend time at his house.

Additionally, my dad would often come into the bathroom when I was on the toilet or in the shower – an activity that was easily explained away by us being a large family in a single-bathroom home. He wore his underwear around the house so that I became accustomed to his partial nakedness, and more than once, he allowed me to walk in on him while he was masturbating. He took me to the theater to see *Pretty Woman,* despite the fact that I was only ten years old, and he often made sexual references in my presence.

All of these behaviors are common grooming methods[5]. They were designed to acclimate me to a sexually abusive atmosphere, to make me feel grown up and mature. He never told me not to tell anyone what he did, but he didn't have to. His grooming behaviors were intentional and, for a while at least, successful.

MYTH: Sexual abuse perpetrators only groom the victim.

FACT: Some abusers, especially those who live outside of the child's home, will intentionally groom the child's parents and caregivers to overlook or ignore the warning signs. As you'll read in Meg's story at the end of the next chapter, her abuser was a friend of her parents. He made himself available to babysit Meg and her sister on a regular basis, for free – a classic grooming behavior[3]. A child predator will often go out of his or her way to appear trustworthy to parents and even the community, to establish a favorable reputation with educators, law enforcement agencies, and government officials. His or her goal is not only to gain access to a child or children, but also to lower the likelihood of the abuse being detected or the child being believed if he or she does disclose it[5].

MYTH: Children do not sexually abuse other children. As such, my child would never abuse another child.

FACT: 40% of sexually abused kids are victimized by an older or stronger child. 23% of all perpetrators are under eighteen[6].

Some will try to diminish the seriousness of sexual activity between kids, perhaps calling it "harmless experimentation." In some cases, that might even be true. Young children, particularly, may engage in sexual behavior without ever recognizing it as wrong or abusive[6]. However, older children may engage a younger, vulnerable child in sexual behavior with the intent to harm or control. Their victims are *not* willing participants, and the trauma the victims experience is genuine.

Erin Merryn, author of *Stolen Innocence: Triumphing over a Childhood Broken by Abuse: A Memoir; Living for Today: From Incest to a Journey of Survival,* and *Healing: A Memoir* has devoted her life to prevention and awareness of child sexual abuse. Her story of rape and abuse began at age six, when she was raped in the home of a friend by the friend's uncle. She was later molested by a male cousin, only a few years older than her, who used violence and threats to keep her quiet. Her story, detailed in *Living for Today,* tells the troubling but not unexpected reaction of the boy's parents when the abuse came to light.

Shock.

Anger.

Disbelief.

The family was torn apart. Erin's parents never doubted their daughter, but the rest of the family – aunts, uncles, extended family – chose to side with the perpetrator. They believed Erin had lied, plain and simple. Despite the closeness between Erin's family and the family of her abuser, despite the fact that Erin had shown no propensity for deception in the past and had therefore given them no grounds to disbelieve her, and even despite the perpetrator's later confession, blaming the victim was a much easier emotional response than confronting the actions of their son and relative.

Through it all, Erin has proven herself to be a woman of great courage. She is the creator of Erin's Law, currently passed in thirty-one states, which requires public schools to provide sexual abuse and assault awareness classes to children from Pre-K through twelfth grade and has already resulted in hundreds of abused children speaking up and getting help. Rather than allow her abuse experience to hinder her, she has used it to literally change the world. She is, however, an exception, especially among those who were abused by another child. Too many others remain silent, continuing to hide their stories and rationalize their ongoing trauma out of fear even decades later.

The following is part of an email from Jan, a woman wrestling with the decision to confront her childhood abuser or to continue her silence to maintain peace in her family.

....

It was a big deal for some reason, to be allowed in his room. I don't remember the circumstances surrounding the first time it happened, what was said or how it progressed. Or even how many times it happened, though it wasn't that many or over too long of a time, I don't think. I know my younger sister also went through something, though I don't know exactly what happened, if hers was during the same time or after mine stopped, or how long it might have lasted. I actually don't remember most of it. Just bits and pieces. It makes my stomach turn to remember the actual touching. I don't remember how we'd get there, just that he was lying down on the bed and I'd be lying down on top of him. He was between my legs and he'd hold my hips still while moving his up and down, rubbing himself on me. I don't remember how it would end, whether he'd finish or just tire of it. That's as far as it went. Nothing more.

I know that somehow I knew it wasn't something to discuss. It was something that happened behind a closed door. A locked door. Closed doors were rare in our house and signified something different was going on. We didn't even close our doors at night when we slept. And we never locked a door. Not even when we left the house.

I know I felt dirty and I didn't like it. I didn't tell, don't think I avoided him otherwise, but certainly was not a willing participant. Maybe that's why it didn't happen often or last long. I don't know.

I want so much to believe that my mom knows nothing of what my brother did to me and my sister. Even now, sitting at my own kitchen table in my own house, almost twenty years removed from that time, bits and pieces I'd so much rather forget are crystal clear. One of them being the loud banging on my brother's locked door once (maybe twice?) and the half-shouted question of why it was locked in the first place. But no questions followed.

And it continued.

I can remember the exact location of the bed within the room: in the far corner, bracketed by the two windows. I can picture it even now though several occupants have lived in the room since, rearranging, painting, hanging new pictures and living different lives there. It was even my room for a short time long after he'd moved out. You'd think that would have bothered me, but I don't know that it even crossed my mind at the time. But the image comes, completely unbidden and unwelcome, and it hasn't changed in my mind. It was the only room in the upper level of the house that had no escape route out either window. My parents commented on it more than once as a fire danger with no porch roof to climb out onto, just a two-story drop to the ground below out both windows. Isolated. Trapped. I remember the dark paneling of the walls before they were painted baby blue. That dark wood look framed a yarn wall hanging that he'd made himself, the bright yellow of a leopard crouching on a tree branch stood in contrast to the dark browns and greens and blacks that give the impression of leaves. That cat sat there, its big, fixed eyes looking out into the room, watching all of the events that happened there. I think it might have been that wall hanging that I saw when I'd turn my head to the side, letting the empty feeling take over as I distanced myself from what was going on, waiting for it to end.

I don't want to remember. I don't want to think about it. I don't want to analyze it or understand it or do anything but forget it and move on. Because if my mom knew then, she knows now and has known all the years in between. And that means she did nothing. Said nothing. All this time. At the time.

That means she still treated him like everything he did in his life was great, like what he had to say really mattered, like he was someone important and something special all the while knowing what he was doing. No matter what I did, I could never come close to comparing to the high opinion she held of him. I could never be what he was to her. We have a tradition in our family – boys are special. Mom would tell me how Gramma had always favored the boys in the family, but it wasn't her fault, really because her mom had done the same. Gramma had grown up in a time when families were large, but babies and young children died often from unknown causes. Several of her brothers had died at very young ages and so it was told to me, it came to be that they wouldn't even name the boys until they'd lived past age two, they were simply called Buddy. And that name is on more than one tombstone in our family plot. So when a boy did live, he was special and was treated that way. Mom would continue her explanation saying that it was just the way Gramma grew up, so it followed logic that she'd be bound to treat her own boys the same way. And as mom would tell me this, she tried to disguise the hurt, but even to a young child it was apparent. She was trying to explain away her own feelings as she made excuses as to why she hadn't been loved the same.

She could see it in her childhood, plain as day, but she was completely blind to it in the way she treated her children. I don't know if she ever saw it the same way. And maybe she didn't really treat my brother differently.

Maybe it's only what I saw and believed at the time, a perception colored by what I'd been told. A self-fulfilling prophecy.

I think this is probably important for me to deal with, to take a close look at what it means and how it might have shaped who I've become. But I don't want to. If I can keep it to myself, discuss it only with people I love and trust to move past it, I think that's doable. But if it means having to dig up ancient history with my family and drag us all through an unthinkably painful encounter that I don't even know the purpose of…I don't know if it's worth it. I don't want to hurt, but I could get through that if necessary. However, I'm not sure that I could knowingly be the cause of hurting others. They live in a small town, a small community. Their lives would be ruined. I fear that this would completely destroy my family if I said something now. I'd be responsible for that.

And why now? Almost twenty years later. What good could possibly come from saying something now? And if I don't bring it up, no one else will. Is it really so essential to know whether she knew or not? It won't change anything. I've learned to deal with it. I don't hate my brother, don't wish him ill. I don't hate my mom, whether she knew what was happening or not. At least, I think that's true. Even if suspicions were awakened, they were never proven. I mean, what parent is going to seek out such an awkward situation, make accusations that, if they aren't true, are embarrassing to say the least, hurtful and damaging at most? Maybe she had no idea what to do, so just waited to see if she'd have to do anything. Maybe she had suspicions, but chose to wait to see if she could figure it out before doing anything. Maybe she just had no idea anything was going on. Who will believe that of their child without being forced to face it?

But. But if she did suspect. If she did know something, anything wasn't right. What kind of parent can take that chance? I'd rather continue believing she knows nothing about it and not have to try to reconcile the good things I know of her with the villain it would seem she would have to be to choose one child over another in that fashion.

She couldn't have known. That's what I so desperately want to hang onto. She couldn't have known and chosen to do nothing. And maybe it's even true. I just want to forget it and go on as we all have been. I can't think of a single good reason to do anything else. At least not anything that requires involving them. So even though I can recognize that it's the coward's way out, I know it's me that has the choice, and, for the time being, I'm making it. And refusing to go past a certain point in this. I'm choosing to stay silent.

....

What Jan does not discuss in this email is the ongoing manner in which her abuse experience affects her life. After several years of marriage, for example, her husband has learned not to try to initiate lovemaking. Sex must be her idea or it cannot happen, so that weeks may pass without a hint of sexual intimacy between them.

She also struggles with shame, convinced, as she is, that her experience does not compare to what other women have gone through and therefore shouldn't cause her any difficulty whatsoever. She believes she should be able to move on, to forget it, to put it behind her. In her mind, the fact that she can't points to some personal flaw or weakness.

As long as Jan compares her story to others and judges herself by that standard, she will not be free to grow and move forward. As long as she continues to deny her pain, she cannot heal. She knows this, yet allows herself to be hindered by her staunch refusal to break her silence. Even though she knows she would not necessarily have to confront her brother or mother in order to heal, the fact that she might is enough to keep her right where she is: in pain, but managing it.

Jan has bought into the final myth, one we've discussed in previous chapters: *sexual abuse should not be a big deal.* The problem, of course, is that it *is* a big deal. It *does* have a lifelong impact. And she, despite her beliefs to the contrary, is worth the temporary emotional and relational hardship that might be caused for herself or her family by overcoming it.

Part III

From Silence to Stories

I can remember the very moment that I became an advocate for sexual abuse prevention and awareness. I was sitting in history class in my second semester of college. At twenty-nine, I was older and more committed to learning than most of the students in the class, but even I couldn't maintain my focus as the professor – an elderly lawyer who interjected the sound "uh" between every phrase, in every sentence, for almost two hours twice a week – droned on and on, making a normally-interesting subject unbearably boring. My mind wandered, and I found myself thinking about my speech class. Semester's end was nearing, and I needed to decide on a topic for my final speech. The assignment stated we could choose from any type of speech we'd learned about in class: informational, persuasive, or instructional. The topic was ours to choose, as well, and while I had had plenty of ideas, none had stuck. I wanted to write my speech about something that mattered, but I didn't know what that would be. So as the professor uhhed and ummed his way through his lecture, I doodled in my notebook and prayed, *Lord, what do You want me to write this speech about?*

Did I expect an answer? I don't know. But it came, so quickly and clearly that I almost looked around to see if someone had spoken it aloud.

Sexual abuse awareness.

I froze in my seat, my heart suddenly beating madly. It was a topic that I had never, ever considered before. I had been telling my story at retreats for quite some time, but the idea of talking about sexual abuse anywhere else had never occurred to me. However, just a few weeks before, we'd learned what had been going on in the home of our friends Steve and Brook. Since then, I'd been plagued with questions: how could we have sat by Steve at church every week, been friends with his family, prayed with him, and not have known that he would do such a thing? What motivates a person to sexually abuse a child? And how many other girls did I know who were secretly being abused?

Every time I spoke at retreats, I shared the statistic I had found regarding the prevalence of sexual abuse: one in four girls is sexually abused before she turns eighteen. Yet, no matter how many times I spoke the words, they'd never seemed real. Now, however, "one in four" were no longer faceless numbers. I knew a "one." Her name was Anna. And suddenly I knew an abuser. Not the memory of my own, not the story of someone else's, but someone in my everyday life who had sexually abused a child. The reality of it had shaken me. Even weeks later I was still reeling, but to write a speech about it?

And deliver it to a class of near strangers?

That didn't seem like something I would do.

Over the next few days I wrestled with the idea. I began to do research even while I convinced myself I'd never follow through. I composed lines even as I told myself to find a different topic. In the end, as you can guess, I delivered that speech – devoid of any reference to my own story – to a class full of stunned faces. At least, I assume their faces were stunned. Mostly I could only see the tops of their heads as they studied their desks, scribbled in their notebooks, or checked their phones – anything, it seemed, but look at me. After it was over, I sat down in the chair next to the podium to gather my materials, my face hidden from the class by a computer, and my professor asked, "How did that feel?"

"Emotional," was all I could reply.

From my hiding place, I heard several chuffs of agreement, but on my way back to my seat, a few caught my eye and nodded or smiled their encouragement. I spent the rest of class in a daze, not even hearing the remaining speeches, as I sorted through what I was feeling. Relief that it was over, for one. Some lingering nerves, like winding down after a shot of adrenaline. But mostly, I felt something I hadn't expected, something I don't think I'd ever felt before.

Accomplishment.

And a sense of purpose, as though the speech was the beginning of something: a future I had not anticipated.

The future, however, often takes longer to arrive than one would hope. I was still almost five years away from graduating. In that five years, I would start a blog about sexual abuse, write essays and short stories about it whenever an assignment allowed it, and chafe that I couldn't do more – no matter that I didn't know what I wanted to do. I had many ideas, some that I developed, others I shelved (and have since forgotten), but no real opportunity to do anything with them. I continued to speak at church retreats for a few more years, but between classes and home-schooling my two middle-schoolers, I eventually had to accept what I couldn't change: all I could do was pray and wait for the next step to become apparent.

Finally, the end of my penultimate semester arrived, and with it the need to choose a project for my senior capstone. My advising professor had told me the best and most practical solution was to do an internship, because it would look good on my resume – important for someone who'd been a stay-at-home mom for seventeen years, and as such didn't have thing to put on a resume. Though it seemed like sound advice, I struggled with the idea. After a couple of weeks of going back and forth, weighing and re-weighing my internal list of pros and cons, I did what I should have done in the beginning. I prayed: *God, what should I do for my capstone project?*

Did I expect an answer? You'd think I would have, after everything. Nevertheless, when the answer came – so swiftly, so clearly – it still surprised me.

Do what I have called you to do. Write.

After that the ideas came fast and strong, and the early vision for this book was born, though at the time I had no idea a book would come out of it. Over the summer and into my final semester, I struggled to put my ideas together, find my writer's voice, and *just start writing already!* By December, however, I had written the required fifty pages: three sections discussing the consequences of silence in a world rife with sexual abuse, and two true survivor stories.

Can you guess what I felt the day I printed out the final draft of that project, encased it in a clear plastic folder, and handed it to my professor?

Accomplishment.

A sense of purpose, as though the project was a part of something important, a future I had long anticipated.

By then I knew I would take those fifty pages and write a book. I knew that I would stay home with our newly-adopted son rather than get a job after graduation like I had always planned (a decision that was made in the now-familiar way: I wrestled with the pros and cons for a few weeks, finally prayed, and felt surprised when I got the answer. Hopefully someday I'll learn to pray first and skip the wrestling altogether). I knew that aside from being Mom to our sweet boy, my only priority would be to write and keep writing until this book was finished.

In doing so, I've struggled with my perceived inadequacies and self-doubt. I've questioned my qualifications to write the stories of women whose abuse experiences are so different than my own. And I've confronted my failures as an advocate, being brought face-to-face, as I have been, with my own silence.

The entire world avoids the subject of sexual abuse. Sometimes even me.

....

Me and Meg

The first time I met Meg, she was crying.

She and I sat around a table with five or six other women, discussing the upcoming retreat we were all attending. Her face was pale as she sat huddled within her heavy sweatshirt, shivering from nerves and suppressed emotion. Meg was a stranger to all of us save one, the friend who had invited her to church just a couple of weeks before. When it came time to introduce ourselves, it was difficult for Meg to do more than say her name. Her friend Gina handled the rest, telling us that she had gotten to know Meg through their sons' soccer team. After becoming friends, Gina invited Meg to church. "When she heard about this retreat, she really wanted to come," Gina said. Meg, never lifting her eyes, only nodded.

After talking a little about the practicalities of the retreat, our group leader asked each of us to share what we were hoping to get out of the weekend. The first couple of answers were vague: "I just want some time away to re-focus," and "I want whatever God has for me." But as we made our way around the table, the women began opening up. One had lost her sister to cancer and was still reeling from the loss; she was hoping to find comfort, solace, and strength to move forward. Another was honest about her battle to overcome her addiction to pornography. The next was a young single mom, struggling with the guilt and shame of her recent divorce. And then it was Meg's turn.

As our eyes fell upon her, we saw a woman who was damaged – so damaged she could no longer hide it from anyone, even a group of strangers. Yet as we watched, she seemed to steel herself against the press of emotions. She sat up straight in her chair, took a deep fortifying breath, and forced the words out through her sobs, "My life is falling apart. My marriage is almost over – and it's all my fault. My kids… the things they've been put through. I just can't live like this anymore."

She stopped then, overcome. Gina wrapped an arm around Meg's shoulders and pulled her close as all the emotion she'd been suppressing poured out. With deep, heaving sobs, Meg's tears fell unchecked. Tears stung my own eyes as I looked away. Her desperation was palpable, her brokenness on display for all to see. It took a few minutes, but the wave eventually subsided. Smiling a little as she took the tissues someone handed her, Meg gestured to the wet spot on Gina's shoulder, saying, "Sorry about your sweater." We all smiled as Gina assured her it was fine, and the tension was broken. Finally, Meg was ready to tell us her story.

She and her husband Devin had been married for three years. They had three children, the oldest of whom was Meg's from her first marriage, and a house in a nice neighborhood. On the outside, their lives looked completely normal, but the truth was different. At age fourteen, Meg had been diagnosed with both bipolar and generalized anxiety disorder. At thirty-one, she continued to struggle with those issues, even to the point of needing several rounds of treatment at an in-patient psychiatric facility. The most recent had been just the month before. She was angry most of the time, and though she directed it toward her husband and children, she recognized that it was with herself she was angry, not them. She hated herself: who she'd been, what she'd done, the person she continued to be in spite of her desire to change. She hated that she put her husband down all the time, for everything, even though he never deserved it. She hated that she had to be in control of everything every minute to keep her anxiety in check. She hated that she had allowed experiences from her childhood to dictate her feelings and actions so many years later.

She told us that she and her older sister were sexually abused for several years by an adult friend of their parents who babysat for them on a regular basis. Her sister, a year and a half older than Meg, herself traumatized by the abuse, went on in later years to molest Meg as well. Meg said she let her sister do it and never told a soul because she "just thought that's what you do, you know? It was normal for us." She only shared it in the group that day because of the way all of it continuously affected her marriage: she hadn't been intimate with her husband since their youngest child, now 18 months old, was conceived. The thought of sex filled her with such disgust and repulsion that she just couldn't do it except when drunk. She'd given up alcohol when she got pregnant and had never picked it up again, fearful of her dependence upon it, but doing so had ruined any chance of physical intimacy between her and her husband.

She was ashamed of the way she felt.

She was also grieved. The upcoming retreat was her and her husband's last-ditch effort to save their marriage, though she didn't think it would help. She felt her marriage was over, and she fully believed it was no one's fault but her own.

Pouring her story out to us at that meeting was the beginning of many firsts for Meg. Over the course of the weekend retreat, she would hear the stories of other sexual abuse survivors, from pastors and leaders to other retreat participants like herself. She would hear women she thought "had it all together," whom she would not have dreamed had ever done anything remotely wrong, talk openly about the choices they made after being sexually abused, some of them the very same choices Meg had made: sexual activity and promiscuity beginning in their early teens, drug and alcohol dependence, addiction to pornography, abortion. Meg heard for the first time how other abuse survivors *felt* about themselves and their abuse: the shame and guilt; the feelings of worthlessness, weakness, and responsibility; the absolute conviction of being irreparably damaged. Meg saw herself in others, identified with their pain, and experienced something she never had before – hope.

Hope of overcoming.

Hope of change.

Hope of living that ever-elusive "normal life."

She felt hope for herself, for her marriage, for the future of her family. In hearing stories of healing from women in every stage of the process – from the very beginning to standing far on the other side, victorious – she realized, *for the very first time*, "That must mean I can heal, too."

Weeks later I heard her husband say of the retreat, "It's like I got my wife back." No longer was Meg angry. No longer did she belittle him or attempt to control everything in their lives. She told me later that she walked away from that retreat feeling like a completely new person. She thought about herself differently, which allowed her to see her husband and her marriage differently, leading to a closeness between them she had never thought possible. She began to wake in the mornings to peace rather than the anxiety and depression she had dealt with for so long. The new sense of peace was so strong, in fact, that she was soon weaned off of all the medications she'd relied on for sixteen years. As I write, it's been nearly a year and she remains symptom-free.

If it were up to me, Meg's story would end right there with her healing and restoration, triumph and freedom. In many ways, it does. Meg and Devin's marriage continues to thrive. Meg continues to grow in emotional and spiritual maturity, amazed and delighted by how far she's come. From the outside, it looks like a real-life fairy tale, like their beautiful family is walking out their blissful happily-ever-after. And they *are*, but it's a relative happily-ever-after. Compared to where they were before, their current state truly is bliss. But what she continues to carry, the weight of it – it's anything but.

When I asked Meg if she would let me tell her story for this project, I had definite expectations of what I would write. I even said to her, "I'm excited to talk with someone who's already on the other side, who has walked out their healing process."

She hesitated a moment, then replied, "Well, who's *trying* to walk it out."

I heard her, but I didn't listen. I was too busy trying to force my preconceived version of her story into a tidy box, easily wrapped with pretty words. A gift of hope to a world of struggling women. I was composing the lines in my head – this beautiful story I just knew I was going to write – as she reiterated what she shared the first night I met her. Was I even listening to her? I think I must not have been. I was so anxious to get to the good part – the healing part – that I shut my ears and eyes to everything that didn't line up with what I wanted to hear. Then she made a statement that stopped me in my thoughtless tracks. She said it calmly, without emotion, as though it was the most normal thing in the world.

Devin and I have just finally learned that we don't have to have sex to be happy.

Over the next few days these lines from Paul Laurence Dunbar's "We Wear the Mask" reverberated in my mind:

> We smile, but, O great Christ, our cries
> To thee from tortured souls arise.
> We sing, but oh the clay is vile
> Beneath our feet, and long the mile;
> But let the world dream otherwise,
>   We wear the mask!

I would read those lines over and over, trying to determine if the joy I had seen in Meg over the last few months truly was a mask – a ruse to hide her still-broken heart – or if her joy was real, a genuine expression of her new-found freedom and healing, despite its being incomplete. I felt grieved by the depth of pain she had kept so well concealed, saddened by her continuing struggle, heartbroken by her resigned acceptance of it.

After a while, I reasoned that the mask she wore was not intentional. The day-to-day lives we must live despite our struggles force the mask upon us, demanding that we put on our happiest face to manage the daily tasks of living. That's understandable, right?

Of course it is.

But as I mulled it over more, I realized that the mask she hides behind is not only forced upon her by the demands of daily living, but also by me and those like me, by our expectations of her story. How happy I was to believe that she had found complete healing in that one weekend retreat. I didn't follow up with her – never even considered it. I heard her testimony of healing from depression and anxiety and assumed that everything else was healed as well. I waited nearly a year to talk to her about it again, a year in which I closed my eyes to any sign that all was not well in her world.

Here's the thing: silence is not always the result of an outright refusal to listen. Sometimes silence feels like necessity, because while you might ask someone how they're doing since their recent back surgery, you are unlikely to ask, "How are you doing since you confronted your childhood trauma?" It just doesn't come up in the course of everyday conversation, right?

So instead, I catch myself thinking, *I'm here if she wants to talk about it.* Because what else *can* I do?

I know that I can be available.

I can be aware.

I can be a safe place for the women in my life to share their stories when they're ready.

And I *do* those things. Being so outspoken about sexual abuse awareness and so passionate about full healing and restoration means that my close friends and I often have conversations about how our experiences have or continue to affect us. We know each other's stories. We know the struggle of processing those stories and the importance of caring for one another's hearts as we walk out our healing. We strengthen one another with our listening ears, prayers, and simple awareness of what the other person's going through.

But not with Meg.

I had not made myself available to her.

I had not been aware of what she was walking through.

I had not shown myself to be a safe place.

Then came the worst realization of all: the mask I had presumed to see had never actually existed at all – except to cover my own eyes. I had become part of "the world [that would] dream otherwise."

Excuse me, Meg, my heart had said. *Please wear the mask.*

All It Takes

B ut sometimes, thankfully, I get it right.

"Have I ever told you my story?"

The question came in a text message from my dear friend Nicky. She and I had been friends about three years, and in that time, we'd gone from mere acquaintances who shared nothing more than a nod or hello when we saw each other at church, to true friends. We had spent plenty of quality time together, and I had shared my story with her in bits and pieces early on. She'd also shared a bit of her story with me, but never in detail. I knew she'd suffered some kind of abuse and neglect, that she'd been in foster care as a young child, and that she'd been adopted by a family member when she was about eleven. I had some suspicions about what she'd been through, but I'd never come right out and asked her to tell me her whole story.

"No, you haven't," I replied. "I've always wanted to ask about it, but I also wanted to wait until you were ready to tell me."

"Okay," she said. "I actually wrote it out some time ago and when you're ready, I want you to read it."

And then she said something that caught my attention in a way that nothing else could. She typed, "Not that I haven't trusted you in the past, but I trust you now. I would like you to know where I've come from and what a work in progress I am."

Those words, they echoed in my mind: Not that I haven't trusted you in the past.

But I trust you now.

Trust.

••••••••••••••••••••••••••••••••••••

A Story about Trust

In February of 2014 we met our son for the first time. He came to us as an 18 month old, a child who'd been in foster care his whole life. Despite his young age, we were his fourth placement. In just the last two months he had been moved twice: from the foster family who'd been his for nearly a year to his mother's home for trial-reunification, and then to us. The case workers, whom he barely knew, brought him by our house at 8:30 in the evening, spent about half an hour telling us a little about his story, and then left, leaving him alone in a house full of strangers.

I had gone to his room to finish getting his bed ready and when I stepped back in, I was struck still by the sight of him: hair too long, clothes too tight, an impossibly small child in a life that was just too big for him to understand. He stood beside the couch, not moving. Just watching.

He wasn't the only one who was struck dumb by the latest turn of events. Less than five hours before we had been a family of four. When a caseworker had called to see if we would be interested in taking placement of an 18-month old boy, I had immediately agreed, but without really believing anything would come of it. A similar call had come about a different child the year before, but then we had been one of three families DHS was considering for placement. They interviewed all three families before deciding to place the child with one of the others. When this call came, I was expecting the same thing again. The caseworker

I spoke with didn't say anything beyond, "Would you be interested in taking placement?" and, "Okay, great! I'll let the worker know."

Ten minutes later – ten minutes I had spent doing normal, every-day things like directing the kids to do their chores and getting ready for the birthday dinner we were going to that evening, looking forward to telling my husband about the phone call from DHS, but wanting to wait until he got home, never dreaming the way our lives were getting ready to change – the phone rang again, a different person this time. "Hi," she said, "this is Shanny with Cherokee Nation Child Welfare. We're on our way to pick the child up right now. We'll take him to the ER for routine physical – nothing to worry about – and then we'll bring him to you. We should be there in, oh, let me see…three hours?"

I spent the next several minutes trying (and failing) to form a coherent sentence. Eventually she took pity on me and my apparent bewilderment and began asking questions about our family, which I answered as best I could, but my brain simply refused to process what was happening. She told me a bit about the little boy's story before asking if I had any questions. I had a hundred, thousands maybe, but not a single one came to mind. I didn't even think to ask his name. We got off the phone with her promise to see me in a few hours.

Whoa.

The evening passed in a rush of practicalities and housework, but then, inexplicably…there he was, little Benjamin. Standing by my couch, scanning the room with his dark eyes, searching for a sign of something – anything – familiar, and finding nothing.

I didn't understand the significance of that. Not yet.

I skipped class the next day (and the next, and as many as I could manage after that) so I could stay home with him. We spent that first day circling each other as two strangers would. I changed his diapers, filled his sippy cup, worked the TV remote. He played with the few toys he'd come with, watched Sesame Street and Curious George, and kept his distance. At nap time he lay down without argument and went right to sleep. In fact, he did everything without argument. If he tried to touch something he wasn't allowed to play with, I only had to say,

"Ben, no," and he'd back away slowly, watching me. I tried throughout the day to get him to sit on my lap or let me play with him and his toys, but he was having none of it. To him I was merely the adult care-giver in his space, Chief Diaper Changer and Baby Bather, and nothing else.

If I'm being honest, it was easy to be that to him. He loved our two teenagers, Tyler and Brenna, and had attached himself to them right away. When they came home from school and for the rest of the evening, they laughed and played with him. He sought out their affection and they showered him with it willingly and joyfully. It was easy to let him be their baby. By then I knew enough about his story to know that he had an out-of-state biological relative who'd shown interest in adopting him, and that she would likely get custody of him whenever all the paperwork was finalized. The caseworkers had told us we would probably have him in our home about six months. I told myself and everyone I talked to that day (and for many weeks after, though it had ceased being true immediately, if it ever had been at all), "We'll just love Ben while we have him, and trust that God will place him according to His plan." I said, "Yes, it'll be hard, but we're just so glad to have the opportunity to be a part of his life, even if it's only for a short time." I was fully committed to loving him while we could and then giving him back.

That idea, noble as it was, lasted a whole day.

I can pinpoint the exact moment everything changed. It was the morning of the second day, and we had gone to visit a friend and her new baby. In this new environment, Ben clung to me, unsure of all the newest people. He sat on my lap for a long time, trying to get comfortable in those unfamiliar surroundings, but soon enough he was playing with the new toys they'd bought for him and munching on the donuts my sister-in-law had brought to bribe his affections. When it was time to go, I put on his coat and he went to the door, saying "Bye-bye!" But I didn't move fast enough for his liking, evidently, because he came back to me and, for the first time, lifted his arms for me to pick him up.

Did time stop in that moment? I remember it like it did. In the snapshot of my memory, I see his earnest face, hands extended toward me in the timeless supplication of childhood, and I remember the thought that would echo in my mind for months afterward:

This child doesn't know me.

He didn't know me, yet he was lifting his arms to me – the least unfamiliar person in a totally unfamiliar world – to pick him up, because, well, what choice did he have? Everything and everyone he knew was gone. The foster parents he'd been with since he was just a few months old; his mother, whom he had been living with for the last few months; every daycare worker and nursery volunteer; even the social workers in charge of his case – they were all gone. He had no control over his circumstances, no way to understand all of the brutal changes in his life. All he could do was lift his arms to this woman he didn't know and hope she'd pick him up.

I understood it then, his absolute vulnerability. And it broke my heart.

Over the next few months I would realize again and again how vitally important trust is to a child. I had always taken it for granted with my own kids, just as they had been fortunate enough to take their trust in me for granted. Tyler and Brenna trusted me because there had never been a time that they *couldn't* trust me. I'd always been there, always taken care of them, always done all of the things that babies and children expect from their moms.

But Ben, uprooted twice in three months, placed in the home of strangers and forced to rely on yet another group of adults he didn't know – he had no one to trust. No one who'd always been there. No one he could know, implicitly and without doubt, would be there when he needed them. When he lifted his arms to me that day, he had done so in the *hope* that I'd pick him up, because he couldn't *know* if I would. Over the next few weeks, he would cry when he fell down in the hope that I'd care enough to comfort him. Then he would fall down again and again just to make sure – would I pick him up every time? Would I hug him close and rub his back every time? If he cried when he was hungry, would I feed him? If he wanted to be held when I was busy, would I put down my textbook and allow him to crawl up into my lap? (The answer was yes, every time, until homework became an impossibility I stopped worrying about. I barely passed my classes that semester, but he was worth every very-low C.)

Benjamin didn't just *know*, like babies should know, that the people in his life truly loved him, so he had to test and try and hope. He had to learn to trust, and he did, but it was slow – so slow! A whole week went by before he'd sit on my lap, and even then only stiffly, refusing to lean into me. It was two months before he would cry when we told him no. (You never think of fit-throwing as a sign of trust until you see a child who doesn't know that he'll still be loved if he acts up.) Three long months passed before he began voluntarily throwing his arms around my neck for a tight hug – all on his own, just because he wanted to, just because he loved me and knew that I would hug him back just as fiercely as he was hugging me. It was nearly four months before he realized that not every woman in his life was called "mama" – because they had been, hadn't they? Foster mom, birth mom, then foster mom again. It follows that babysitters and sisters and grandmothers must be "mama," too.

The months between February, when he arrived on our doorstep, and October, when the judge ruled he would never have to leave us, were the most difficult and most beautiful of my entire life. Beautiful because my mornings were spent watching YouTube videos of annoying kids' songs and looking up pictures of animals on Google so that he could learn to say "bear" and "wolf" and "sloth." Beautiful because the splendor of every smile and belly laugh and new word was magnified, like the glory of a million suns shone in his sweet face, and I was dazzled beyond words.

But hard, harder than anything I'd encountered before, because I was living in a deserted place where nothing but fear and sometimes outright panic thrived. When people asked me if we would get to keep him, I would recite my standard line: "The case workers said we'll probably have him about six months, just until his great-aunt gets done with her paperwork and training." Of our possible-impending loss, they would inevitably say the same thing: "I don't know how you do it." I would smile then and say the right thing about faith and trust and prayers for God's perfect will to be done.

On the inside, however, I was terrified by the unknown, by our lack of control, and by the very real possibility that we would have to pass this sweet boy – our *son* – off to yet another stranger, breaking his heart and ours in the process.

One day he took off down the hallway, chasing after the older two, yelling, "Bye, Mama!" and it almost broke me because of how easy it had become for him to say "bye bye." He knew by then that every goodbye was temporary; whether it was he or I that was leaving, he'd learned to trust that we would be together again very soon. How to explain to a barely-two-year old that someday we might not be?

Another night I laid in bed crying – sobbing really – begging God for an answer because I could no longer stand the *not knowing*. Would we get to keep him forever? Would the case workers show up out of the blue one day to take him? (I knew this was a highly unlikely scenario because of placement protocols, but since when is melodrama rational?) Would we survive the loss if they did?

I knew from experience and from the promises in the scriptures that we would make it through if our sweet Ben did leave us, but I knew that losing him would bring a season of grief like we'd never known. I imagined trudging through those days – heart broken, arms empty – in a joyless fog. I imagined dragging my bruised and broken body across a rocky desert, bleeding, weeping, exhausted. Surviving yet broken.

I lived in fear of it every day.

It took Ben four months to learn to trust us to be his family, but it took me more than six – six long months of fear and anxiety and turmoil – to learn to truly trust God. I had been saying all the right things about faith and prayer and God's will, but the mountain of fear I lugged with me everywhere belied my words. I didn't trust God to protect my heart, to hold it tenderly in his hands; I expected Him to stand by wordlessly, unmoved, as it was crushed by loss. I didn't trust Him to preserve Ben's precious heart; I expected Him to carry out

His arbitrary will at the expense of every broken life who might wish differently.

But God, like love, suffers long and is kind. He is not provoked, and He keeps no record of wrongs. He loves us with an everlasting love that is not and *cannot* be thwarted by the weaknesses of our humanity. He is determined, against all odds, to carry, comfort, and provide for us in spite of ourselves. The change was painfully slow, but He patiently spoke truth to me until I could live every day and rest every night with my heart (where my faith lived) and my soul (where my emotions ruled) in agreement. Me, my family, our sweet Benjamin – we were safe in His hands.

Trust, I learned, brings peace – just like it had for Benjamin, and just like it did for me.

And with peace comes a willingness to lift our arms, expose our vulnerability, and allow someone to carry us.

....

"Thank you," I told my friend, Nicky. "I would truly love to read your story." And read it, I did: the story of a young girl, abused and misused and taken advantage of, who spent years in the foster care system and in the care of relatives who did little to protect her heart and body. It's the story of a young woman, heart guarded behind a thick-walled fortress, finding the courage to be open and honest about who she is, one trusted friend at a time. It is a tragic and beautiful story that begins with a broken family and ends in the middle with a strong woman, growing stronger, walking away from her past and toward freedom from it.

I did not set out to earn Nicky's trust. I didn't set out to scale the walls she hid behind – I honestly wasn't aware they existed. I just knew I wanted to be her friend, and friendship, like all relationships, requires three things: availability, awareness, and safety. As I became available to her – to go to breakfast, to answer text messages, to hug her when we met in the halls of the church – I became aware of her broken places. And with that awareness came the desire, and then the follow through, to become a safe place for her. In response, she felt safe enough to share her story with me, to reach out and reveal her vulnerability, and in doing so took a step – not her first nor her last, but *another* step – toward healing.

And that, from all of us, is all it takes.

Afterword

To the reader who has courageously read every word of this book from the beginning to now: thank you. I hope and pray that what you've read has impacted your life in a positive way, despite the difficult moments you've surely endured along the way.

To the reader who read the first couple of chapters, then skipped to the end because *Oh my God, this book is awful*: I don't blame you. Really. Thank you for trying, and I hope and pray that someday you will pick it up again, and perhaps make it a little farther that time.

When I started this project, I had no idea what it would become. I didn't know what to say or how to say it or if I had the courage to say it either way. Even after hearing the first story, I was lost. My heart was stirred, but I just couldn't imagine how the vision I had could translate into a completed capstone project, much less a book. I wanted to write something like I'd never seen before. Not a memoir. Not a self-help, *this-is-how-I-found-healing* treatise. I didn't want to write only for the abuse survivor who may still be struggling (the common audience for books about sexual abuse), but also for the person who was never abused, the person who has no way to identify with an abuse survivor. The person who, like my husband for so many years, didn't understand the lasting consequences of sexual abuse that a survivor will most certainly deal with to some degree. In Jim's case, he knew what had happened to me (in the most general terms) but he never understood how it had affected me. He didn't realize that the issues we'd dealt with consistently in our marriage were tied to it. I wanted to write something that would help others like him understand the abuse survivors in their lives.

Then after hearing the first friend's story, I understood that sometimes even abuse victims don't realize that what they deal with is common to sexual abuse survivors. And I saw that, unless they have a strong network of support, these women may never feel free to speak of their experiences – for so many reasons. They may never find the freedom that comes with shedding the weight of countless secrets, with throwing off the lies and shame that paralyze them into silence. I wanted to write something that would inspire survivors to exchange their silence for stories – *their* stories, shouted from the rooftops or whispered to a trusted friend – because silence is heavy, but stories, once released, float out into the world and join other stories until everyone, everywhere, is in agreement: child sexual abuse is a tragedy that must be denied no longer.

Now I have. Or I have at least tried my very best.

It's a prospect that in turn terrifies and amazes me.

This book you hold in your hands the substance of a dream – a scary, impossible dream that sanity itself says is a terrible idea, one that I doubted and fought and prayed ceaselessly over because I knew it could be completed no other way. What happens next is up to you. Will you, sexual abuse survivor, tell your story? Perhaps, in the course of reading this book, you have already. Whether you have or want to or have no intention of ever doing so, know that I'm praying for you: for your healing, for your freedom, and that your story, in all its simplicity and complexity, will change your world.

And to you, reader, who bravely picked up this book and read to the end despite never having been sexually abused yourself, you who are perhaps just now becoming aware of the impact sexual abuse has on its victims and society, will you now choose to see the world differently? Will you be vigilant to protect the children in your life as far as your realm of influence allows? Will you encourage the survivors in your life to tell their stories?

I pray that you will. I pray that you are bold enough, brave enough, to confront the tragedies in your world rather than hiding from them – pretending them away – as all of us would rather do.

And finally to you, courageous reader, whether you are a sexual abuse survivor or not: Will you make yourself available to the survivors in your life? Will you be aware of their journey? Will you be a safe place for them to stop and rest along the way? I pray that, if nothing else, this book has helped you to realize that healing and freedom are possible – but not if we perpetuate the silence. Not if we keep a death grip on the status quo and refuse, for the sake of our own imagined comfort, to speak.

As individuals, as churches, as communities, and as a society, we *can* grow. We can elicit change. We can break the cycle of sexual abuse for the benefit of every generation that follows. As I said before, we must only begin. And I pray, more than anything else, that you *will* begin. Tell your story. Hear someone else's. Be available, be aware, and be a safe place for the women in your life to exchange their silence for stories.

About the Author

Emily Getzfreid is a wife, mother, friend, and womens ministry leader at DestinyLife Church. She earned her undergraduate degree in English with a minor in Social Welfare from Northeastern State University. Emily enjoys volunteering with various ministries including Don't Look Back, a local prison ministry, and Stand in the Gap (SITGM. org). She lives in Claremore, OK, with her husband and three children.

Emily would like to dedicate this book to her friend Tierney, without whom not a single word would have been written. Out of respect for her friend's modesty, she put this dedication in the back, but Tierney's contributions of love, encouragement, and technical expertise are evident on every page. Emily would also like to say a special thank you to her husband, Jim, and to all the women who contributed their stories for this book.

References

[1] Vilenica, Sheryle, Jane Shakespeare-Finch, and Patricia Obst. "Exploing The Process Of Meaning Making In Healing And Growth After Chilhood Sexual Assault: A Case Study Approach." Counselling Psychology Quarterly 26.1 (2013): 39-54. Academic Search Premier. Web. 27 Sept. 2014.

[2] Steele, William, and Malchiodi, Cathy A. Trauma-Informed Practices with Children and Adolescents. Routledge Taylor & Francis Group: New York. 2012.

[3] American Humane Association. "Child Sexual Abuse." *AmericanHumaneAssociation.org.* n.d. web.

[4] Child Molestation Research and Prevention Institute. "An Ongoing Sex Drive Directed Toward Children: What Causes Someone to Molest?" *Childmolestationprevention.org.* 2016. Web.

[5] The National Center for Victims of Crime. "Grooming Dynamics." *VictimsofCrime.org.* 2012. Web.

[6] Parents Protect! "Abuse Among Children and Young People." *ParentsProtect.co.uk.* n.d. Web.

[7] Ahearn, Laura A. "How Can I Protect My Child from Sexual Assault?" n.d. Parents for Megan's Law. Web. 2/09/2013

CPSIA information can be obtained
at www.ICGtesting.com
Printed in the USA
BVHW032145110322
631324BV00005B/252